WATERLOGGED WEALTH

Why waste the world's wet places?

by
Edward Maltby

WITHDRAWN

© Earthscan 1986
ISBN No. 0-905347-63-3

Published by the International Institute for Environment and
Development, London and Washington, DC.

Typeset and printed by Russell Press, Nottingham, UK.

Cover drawing and design by Robert Purnell. Farmers in the Marais
Poitevin in western France have for centuries used the marshes as a
transport route for themselves, their harvests and their cattle.

This book was edited by John McCormick and Lloyd Timberlake, and
produced by Barbara Cheney.

Earthscan is an editorially-independent news and information service
on global development and environment issues. Part of the
International Institute for Environment and Development, it is
financially supported by several UN agencies, the European
Community, the Nordic aid agencies (DANIDA, FINNIDA, NORAD
and SIDA), the Netherlands Foreign Ministry, the World Bank, the
Swedish Red Cross, the Fondation de France and the Technical Centre
for Agricultural & Rural Cooperation (CTA).

Waterlogged wealth was produced with the advice, cooperation and
financial assistance of the World Wildlife Fund (WWF) and the
International Union for Conservation of Nature and Natural Resources
(IUCN). Any comments or opinions expressed in the book are
however solely those of the author, and should not be taken to
represent the views of WWF, IUCN or of any other funding agencies.

It is published in support of the WWF/IUCN Wetlands Conservation
Programme 1985-87.

Acknowledgements

Many individuals have wittingly or unwittingly assisted in my writing of this book and there is insufficient space to mention them all. I should like to thank colleagues at the Centre for Wetland Resources, Louisiana State University for the many hours of stimulating argument in the laboratory and at various international venues, especially Eugene Turner who first introduced me to Baton Rouge, and new concepts about wetlands; James Gosselink, John Day, Irv Mendelsohn, William Patrick and Stephen Faulkner. Part of the text was written in Louisiana and I thank Bob and Elaine Allen for their hospitality and inspiring company. Compilation of the text would have been impossible without earlier discussions and interest of many wetland scientists, managers, ecologists and geographers throughout the world — Curtis Richardson, Frank Klötzli, Brij Gopal, Joseph Larson, Donald MacIntosh, Gary Hendrix, Bill Trimble, Dennis Whigham, Sven Bjork, Nigel Wace, Bernard Clement, Charles Shier, Keith Thompson, Arnold van der Valk and Leonard Curtis. I hope the many others will excuse lack of mention by name.

Pat Dugan at IUCN provided much useful information and comment on the text and discussion and Derek Scott at IWRB gave generously of his time in ensuring that the most up-to-date material about the Neotropics was available.

Thanks are due to Professor Leendert Pons for reading and correcting sections on acid soils in the Mekong, to Professor Frederik Pannier for providing additional information on Venezuela and Dr Ted Hollis for access to unpublished reports on Tunisian wetlands.

It would not have been possible to impart information on the world's wetlands in the perspective attempted here without considerable international travel. I am grateful to the many bodies who have made this possible financially, especially the Royal Society, the British Council, US Army Corps of Engineers and the University of Exeter Research Fund. Periods of absence from the University have been generously granted and the forbearance of colleagues in the Geography Department much appreciated. Without the stimulating atmosphere and technical support of the department there would be no possibility of empirical studies. Professor Allen Straw and Professor William Ravenhill are thanked for advice on specific parts of the text.

Terry Bacon, Rodney Fry and John McCormick drew the figures, Gaye Napier assisted with some of the initial literature search and my wife, Rosemary, undertook fieldwork, suggested the title, and mastered new word processing technology to convert my scribble to legibility into many of the early hours.

John McCormick and Lloyd Timberlake edited the manuscript; their help and industry has made the text much more readable but remaining errors and limitations are my own.

EDWARD MALTBY

Author's dedication

For
Rosemary, Alistair, Peter and Geoffrey

Contents

Foreword

In 1974, the World Food Conference pledged to end hunger within 10 years. Sadly, we are today further than ever from achieving that goal. Increased population, and continuing degradation and reduced productivity of our natural ecosystems are occurring side by side, particularly in developing countries.

Despite that, there is cause for hope. Governments and development agencies are looking again at their use of the natural environment, recognising that mistakes have been made and seeking new and innovative solutions for the future. But this is a slow process. To date, the world's attention has focused only on a few major habitats or regions, tropical rain forests and the Sahel being the most topical examples. Yet for development to be truly sustainable, environmental awareness must spread to other habitats and regions.

Wetlands are among the most productive — and most threatened — ecosystems. The marshes, swamps and floodplains upon which were founded the great civilisations of ancient Egypt, Mesopotamia and Indo-China, and which continue today to support rural communities throughout the world, are menaced by drainage, reclamation and pollution. Many have already been lost.

It is sadly ironic that as we have sought to exploit the riches of these habitats, we have unwittingly destroyed them. Unconscious of their fragility we have, in our attempt to increase productivity, so disturbed the natural system that productivity has declined in several places. Yet if we are to feed our growing population we must try again to utilise these wetland resources. We must not only harvest their natural production, but also examine their potential for agriculture and aquaculture. Similarly, if we are to reduce our dependence upon hydrocarbon fuels we must also consider the potential of many rivers for generation of hydropower.

But as Dr Maltby argues, we should approach these questions in a way which takes account of the complexities and value of the ecosystems which we seek to exploit. Development should take account of the ecological structure of these systems if we are to continue to reap benefits from them on a sustainable basis.

As he emphasises in *Waterlogged wealth*, the wetlands record of the developed world is not a proud one. Only now are these countries beginning to appreciate the full value of wetlands which have been drained, dammed and destroyed in the search for short-term profit. Developing nations must learn from costly northern mistakes, many of which are documented here. Developing economies cannot afford to repeat these mistakes.

By learning from past mistakes and working to develop further our understanding of the benefits which wetlands provide, we can hopefully conserve them for the benefit of present and future generations. This message must come across loudly and clearly to the governments, aid agencies, and other decision-makers who hold the future of our environment in their hands. This book seeks to achieve this goal. All of us who are concerned with the sound management of our natural environment as a basis for sustainable development will do well to give it our full support.

M.S. Swaminathan
President, IUCN

Introduction

Wetlands are wastelands; that, at least, is the traditional view. Words like marsh, swamp, bog and fen imply little more than dampness, disease, difficulty and danger. Such apparent waste can only be put to good use if the wetlands are 'reclaimed' for agriculture or building.

Nothing could be further from the truth. Far from being wastelands, they are among the most fertile and productive ecosystems in the world. They are essential life-support systems, play a vital role in controlling water cycles, and help to clean up our environment.

Some wetlands can produce up to eight times as much plant matter as an average wheat field, promising higher crop yields if the fertility of wetland soils can be harnessed and the ecosystem managed to give sustained production. They hold great promise for aquaculture: farmers in the southern United States have been experimenting with raising crayfish and timber, or crayfish and rice, in the same ponds — with encouraging results.

Many coastal wetlands support fisheries worth millions of dollars. The Wadden Sea of northern Europe acts as a major nursery area for valuable North Sea fish. About two-thirds of US shellfish and commercial and sports fisheries rely on coastal marshes for spawning and nursery grounds. In the inner delta of the Niger River in northern Mali, wetland fisheries provide a livelihood for 10,000 families and earn $5 million a year.

Wetlands sift dissolved and suspended materials from floodwaters, thereby encouraging plant growth, and prevent the water becoming over-rich in nutrients and poor in oxygen. They also filter sediments and pollutants out of water, maintaining water quality. Wetland plants like the water hyacinth are so efficient at cleaning sewage that they are being used in waste water treatment systems. One marsh in Wisconsin in the United States has been purifying domestic sewage since 1923.

By absorbing floodwater and acting as barriers against surges of storm water, wetlands protect coasts and inland areas from floods, reducing the dangers posed to people and agriculture. Nearly 70% of the land subject to severe flooding in the United States is agricultural land, much of it drained wetland.

Wetlands are among the last truly wild and untouched places on earth. Many are vital breeding and nursery grounds for waterfowl and animals, and support plants that are — or could be — of use to man. The wetlands of the northern US and Canada together provide nesting and breeding grounds for about two-thirds of North America's breeding ducks. Life itself may have begun in the shallow protein-rich waters of some ancient coast. The boundary between land and water was the single most important barrier to the evolution of organisms capable of life out of the water. Great civilisations were born out of wetlands in the floodplains of the Nile, the Tigris-Euphrates and the Indus.

Wetlands cover 6% of the world's land surface, and are found everywhere, in all climates and countries, from the tundra to the tropics. Yet few people really know what they are. The word 'wetland' does not even appear in dictionaries. This ignorance — bordering on fear of the most desolate and apparently hostile swamps and bogs — is the single major cause of their destruction. Wetlands everywhere are under threat. For centuries, notes David Baldock, director of Britain's Earth Resources Research Ltd, "the drainage of wetlands has been seen as a progressive, public-spirited endeavour, the very antithesis of vandalism".

Opening new land to agriculture is the most common argument for reclamation, and the major threat to wetlands. In the United States, 87% of recent wetland losses have been to agriculture; between the 1950s and the 1970s, US wetland losses were running at 185,000 hectares a year. In the Third World, the urgent need to feed people is a convincing argument in favour of draining wetlands. But while drainage may increase local yields in the short term, in the long term it may cut the ability of a wetland to produce its own sustained harvests. A major drainage and flood control scheme in Jamaica, for example, threatens local fisheries and breeding grounds for waterfowl, fish and shrimp.

Dams and barrages, built to provide power and irrigation, often do so only at the cost of downstream floodplain fisheries and wildlife habitat. An uncertain future awaits the 100,000 semi-nomadic fishermen downstream of 11 new dams planned for the Niger; 90% of Mali's total fish catch is at risk.

The Sundarbans forest of India and Bangladesh, one of the most important refuges for the Bengal tiger, has gradually deteriorated over the past decade as the flow of the Ganges has been reduced by barrages. Construction of the Jonglei Canal in southern Sudan — meant to provide water for Egypt and the Sudan — could compromise a wetland that supports 750,000 head of cattle, the livelihoods of Nuer and Dinka herders, and hundreds of thousands of mammals and birds.

Their real importance is only now being understood by scientists and planners, who freely admit their ignorance about how wetlands function, and about how they interconnect with their wider environment. Changes in one locality can have knock-on effects hundreds or even thousands of kilometres away, often in another country.

Wetlands are the only ecosystem type that have their own international convention — the Ramsar convention of 1971, under which signatories agree to include wetland conservation in their national planning and to promote their sound utilisation. But there is often a chasm between this rhetoric and actual policy. Signatories are required to list only one wetland, even when they may have others that are worth conserving. Progress is hampered — as it so often is — by lack of finance.

Developed countries have apparently not yet learned from their centuries of experience. Wetland conversion and drainage goes ahead despite uncertainty about what benefits *might* come from more carefully considered management and exploitation. The Irish peat board argues that any ecological damage brought about by peat mining in Ireland is a small price to pay for reduced import bills and an improved standard of living.

The same mistakes are being repeated in the developing world, where many of the biggest wetland conversion projects in the Third World are being carried out with foreign aid. The Netherlands — which has a longer history of expertise in land drainage than most other countries — has financed drainage surveys in Zambia and Jamaica. Swedish and Finnish funding is supporting a prospective peat mining project in Jamaica, and Japanese money is going into a plan to drain Jamaican wetlands for agriculture.

Non-governmental organisations have a major role to play in lobbying for the wise use of development funds and for more care in the management of wetlands. In 1985, the World Wildlife Fund and IUCN launched a campaign aimed at promoting better public awareness about wetlands and their importance. A major goal of the campaign is to ensure that wetland development goes ahead only when all the implications are understood, and when plans have been made to ensure that the environmental consequences are minimised.

Many wetlands already have been lost irretrievably. Many more are under immediate threat. Attitudes to wetlands are changing, but not fast enough. Wetland conservation must become part of development policy, in both North and South. There is no longer time simply to talk about wetland conservation. Civilisation began around wetlands; today's civilisation has every reason to leave them wet and wild.

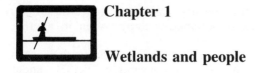

Chapter 1

Wetlands and people

Wetlands provide people — directly and indirectly — with an enormous range of goods and services: staple food plants, fertile grazing land, support for coastal and inland fisheries, flood control, breeding grounds for waterfowl and fuel from peat, among others.

Many of these products are a direct result of the extraordinary productivity of wetland communities. Like all plants, wetland plants use solar energy in photosynthesis to fix carbon and accumulate chemical energy. But they do it particularly well. Ugandan papyrus marsh and sub-tropical saltmarsh can be twice as productive as lush tropical rainforest. Unfertilised papyrus growing in an African wetland can produce the same amount of plant matter as maize receiving heavy doses of fertiliser [1]. Cattail and reed marsh may produce four or five times as much plant matter per unit area as, for example, the grasslands of the US Midwest.

Wetland plants are highly productive in waterlogged conditions that would damage or kill the roots of other plants. Many have specialised tissue or organs through which oxygen can be moved quickly to the roots. Many have large leaf areas and little wood or thickened tissue, meaning that more of a wetland plant is devoted to photosynthesis — to creating energy and growth — than in many land plants. Most are perennials; the fact that they do not die off each year allows more effective storage and efficient use of nutrients. Some wetland plants have odd physiological adaptations, such as the ability to stimulate alcoholic fermentation in roots to provide energy, at the same time avoiding alcohol poisoning.

The environmental 'mechanics' of wetlands adds to their productivity. Most wetland soils are alternately wetted and dried. This increases the release of nutrients and speeds the turnover of organic matter. Water moving past the plants, especially in tidal wetlands, provides a steady or pulsed supply of nutrients, even though the nutrient concentration in the water may be low. This water movement removes dead tissue, keeping plant communities healthy and vigorous. Finally — and most obviously — wetland plants in healthy wetlands rarely suffer from lack of water.

But does this high production matter in the least, when the material produced is 'worthless'? Who eats papyrus? In fact, the high productivity of wetlands is important to humans on two counts.

* First, a wetland can and does produce a high sustainable yield of plants with direct uses to humans.
* Second — and more significantly — a wetland can support other plants and animals through grazing and food chains, both within the wetland itself and beyond its boundaries through the action of currents and tides. It is this 'hidden' value that is too often forgotten in the calculations of planners.

Important plant harvests

Many wetland plants are economically important; some are food staples. Rice — most of which is grown in flooded soils — is the primary food resource of over half the world's people, and occupies 11% of all arable land. Oil palm, a tree originating in West African wetlands, is one of the world's most important sources of edible and soap-making oil. It yields more oil per hectare per year than any other vegetable and more oil than can be obtained from the fat of animals raised on the same area [2]. Breeding has extended the plant to drier and drier environments.

Less well known — but no less important — is sago palm. The swamp sago (*Metroxylon sagu*) is an important component of the floodplain swamps of southeast Asia. The pith of the palm produces a starch from which sago flour is made. Sago is the main food staple for a quarter of the population of Irian Jaya (the Indonesian section of the island of Papua New Guinea) and over 100,000 Papuans [3].

Many of the vast swamps of Indonesia and elsewhere in southeast Asia are suitable for sago cultivation. The high yield of starch (generally 7-9 tonnes per hectare per year but possibly as much as 30 tonnes per hectare) opens up exciting prospects for producing large amounts of food with little environmental impact.

Awareness of the food and raw material potential of sago has led the Japanese — in their search for raw materials to supply the nation's growing starch conversion industry — to form the Sago Palm Research Sub-Committee. Through bioconversion (using microorganisms as chemical converters), sago can be used to produce either alcohol or protein. Recent trials suggest that it may be possible to convert 14.5 tonnes of starch (a reasonable yield for one hectare) into 3.5 tonnes of protein [4]. Hence there may be advantages in cultivating high-yield starch plants like sago in little-disturbed wetlands, rather than draining swamps at great expense to plant crops richer in protein but with much lower yields.

Rice paddies in Cibodas, Indonesia. Wetlands are a source of economically important food plants. Rice — a wetland plant — is the major food staple of over half the world's people.

Tom Moss/WWF

Wetlands are a major source too of non-food plants. Reeds (mainly *Phragmites* spp.) are used in thatching, paper production and, in some places, bedding. In tropical swamplands the fronds of palms like the Bull Thatch (*Sabal jamaicensis*) in Jamaica and the mangrove palm (*Nypa fruticans*) in the Philippines and Indo-Pacific region are used extensively for roofing. High-yielding crops of willow (*Salix* spp.) are still grown in the Somerset Levels of southwest England to supply the raw materials for basket weaving.

In Czechoslovakia, a hectare of land can produce yields of 100-350 bundles of reed (1.5m long and 1m in circumference) per hectare [5]. Over 30 million hectares of US commercial forests (excepting Alaska and Hawaii) are in swamps or on land subject to periodic flooding. Plantations of eastern cottonwood on the Mississippi floodplain are producing five times the yield of the natural bottomland hardwoods [6].

Bald cypress is a durable, strong and lightweight timber much sought after in the US construction industry. Nearly all the original stands have long been cleared in the southern United States, but second growth stands can produce 425 cubic metres per hectare. The timber is now so highly valued that 19th Century homes in the South are being stripped and their timber re-used. Cypress planting has been advocated recently not just to maintain wetlands but as sound forestry economics [7]. One company — the St Martin Land Company — has recently been planting cypress in aquaculture ponds near Henderson, Louisiana, creating interesting possibilities for harvesting both wood and protein out of the same ecosystem.

Mangrove products. Mangroves (e.g. *Ceriops* and *Avicennia*) yield highly durable wood ideal for poles and pilings in nearby communities. But the use of mangrove wood is by no means restricted to mangrove areas.

* The Japanese produce rayon fibre from several mangrove species in southeast Asia.
* The Philippines, Indonesia and Thailand export over a million cubic metres of chipwood yearly to Japan, worth over $15 million [8].
* In the Sundarbans swamp forests of coastal Bangladesh, many coastal communities are sustained through harvesting firewood and producing honey and wax directly from mangroves.
* Mangrove bark contains 20-30% tannin — used in tanning leather — and extracts are used extensively in the leather industry, in medical treatments and in the wine and beer industry. In the Philippines the sap of *Exoecaria agallocha* is used to deaden nerves in dental cavities.
* The mangrove palm (*Nypa fruticans*) variously provides fodder, fuel, alcohol, vinegar and sugar. Wild nipa swamp, which often appears inland of the mangrove coastal fringe, can yield three tonnes per hectare of sugar [9].

Food chains: grazing and debris

The dry matter and nutrients in wetland plants enter food chains either when plants are directly grazed or when they are broken down and their remains used as food.

The consumption of living plants is essential not only for the survival of plant-eating species — and so of the natural ecosystems of which they are part — but for the survival of human societies dependent on grazing animals. Among the many economically important wild animals which feed extensively on wetland vegetation are: waterfowl; fur-bearing mammals such as muskrat and coypu (a beaver-like rodent originally native to South America); game species such as caribou, moose, lechwe (an African antelope) and capybara (a South American rodent related to the guinea pig); and the remarkable but increasingly rare manatees of tropical rivers and estuaries.

Direct products

FUEL

Firewood for cooking, heating, smoking fish, smoking sheet rubber, and burning bricks; charcoal, and alcohol.

CONSTRUCTION

Timber for scaffolds and heavy construction, railway ties, mining pit props, boat building, dock pilings, fence posts, water pipes, chipboards, and flooring and panelling; beams and poles for buildings; and thatch or matting.

FISHING

Poles for fish traps, fishing floats, fish poison, tannins for net and line preservation, and fish-attracting shelters.

TEXTILES

Synthetic fibres, dye for cloth, and tannins for leather preservation.

FOOD, DRUGS and BEVERAGES

Sugar, alcohol, cooking oil, vinegar, medicines from bark, leaves and fruits, tea substitute, fermented drinks, dessert topping, condiments, sweetmeats, and vegetables.

HOUSEHOLD ITEMS

Furniture, glue, hairdressing oil, tool handles, rice mortar, toys, matchsticks, and incense.

AGRICULTURE

Fodder and green manure.

PAPER PRODUCTS

Paper, and packing boxes.

Indirect products

Fish, prawns, shrimps, crab, oysters, mussels and cockles for food.

Bees for honey and wax.

Birds for food, feathers and recreation.

Mammals for food, fur and recreation.

Reptiles for skins, food and recreation.

Recreational uses

Power-boating, canoeing, fishing, collecting molluscs and crustaceans, hunting, hiking, picnicking, swimming and snorkeling, birdwatching, wildlife observation, photography, and nature education.

Products of the mangrove ecosystem. Source: Saenger 1984 and Hamilton and Snedaker 1984.

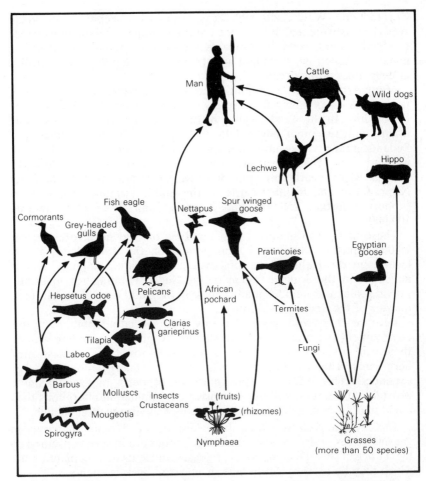

Generalised food web on the Kafue Flats of Zambie. Source: adapted from Handlos 1982 in Drijver & Marchand 1985.

Some fish are predominantly herbivorous. *Tilapia* species account for over half the fish biomass of Botswana's Okavango delta. The three-spot bream feeds mainly on algae and other small organisms, and the red-breasted bream lives mainly on green plants. A major part of the 400 tonnes of fish annually taken from the delta depends on the energy fixed by wetland plants.

The grazing chain. Large numbers of domestic livestock are grazed on wetlands. Grazing marshes once covered 1.5 million hectares of lowland

England and Wales; although large areas of European and North American grazing marsh have been drained, large numbers of livestock still feed in summer on the remnants of coastal saltmarsh and floodplain marshes. Indeed the rich plant life of these areas depends on controlled grazing and cutting cycles.

Many African rural communities survive by moving their cattle — and their crops — as falling floodwaters expose enriched bottomlands and floodplains. In the middle valley of the Senegal River in Senegal and Mauritania, the inner Niger delta in Mali, and the Jonglei region of Sudan's great Sudd swamp, perhaps 1.5 million people depend on this wetland cycle. Their herds are large: over two million head along the Senegal River; nearly three million cattle, sheep and goats on the Inner Niger delta; and 800,000 cattle in the Sudd. Zambia's Kafue Flats support a further 250,000, and Kenya's Tana River delta another 100,000.

These lands also maintain vast numbers of wild herbivores: nearly 10,000 topi, waterbuck and hippopotami on the Tana delta; 50,000 lechwe on the Kafue Flats; and over half a million animals, mainly antelope, in the Jonglei region of the Sudd. Hunting for meat still provides much protein for many tribes; in the Sudd it may account for a quarter of the animal meat intake.

Because many wild species have evolved special adaptations to this environment (such as the lechwe's ability to graze in standing water), they can graze more efficiently on wetlands than domesticated herbivores. That is, they can assimilate more energy for less energy expended. This offers the possibility of properly managed wildlife providing more food without expensive environmental alterations than could many farming systems which produce environmental change.

The detritus pathway. Microbes consume dead plant materials in various stages of decomposition. The microbes are in turn consumed by higher organisms. Decomposition releases nutrients held in plant tissue, which may be used by consumers or recycled back to plants.

This 'detritus cycle' couples wetland and aquatic food chains, making wetlands a key link in the support of both freshwater and coastal fisheries. But the complexity of detritus food chains makes it difficult to determine exact levels of energy and nutrient support or the precise links involved.

Nevertheless, work in the harsh environment of the Arctic coastal plain has emphasised the reality of the link. Here it has been found that freshwater organisms depend partially on peat detritus. The food chain stretches not only from organism to organism, but far back into the past. Carbon from plants and animals fixed into the peat thousands of years previously passes through insect larvae and other small organisms, eventually to fish and ducks. Radiocarbon dating of the tissues of the fish and ducks can produce surprising results: one specimen of Oldsquaw duck (*Clangula hyemalis*) showed a radiocarbon age of 1,300 years. While this had little to do with the age of the duck, it reflected the *average* age of the carbon entering the duck's body at the time of the testing [10].

The Grand Lac of the Mekong, reputed to be one of the most productive freshwater fisheries in the world, owes its status to seasonal flooding in its wetland margins, which brings organic matter into the lake from the vegetation on the flooded plain [11].

Fisheries

Coastal, lake and floodplain wetlands are highly productive spawning, nursery and feeding areas for fish. Not only are they a rich food base, but they protect young fish from strong currents, sunlight and predators. About two-thirds of major US commercial fisheries (and 90% of those in the Gulf of Mexico) depend on estuaries and saltmarshes as nursery and spawning grounds. The yield of fish and shellfish dependent on wetlands was worth over $700 million in 1976. Two-thirds of the fish caught worldwide are hatched in tidal areas.

Coastal wetlands and estuaries encourage the settling out of particles of organic matter and nutrients which may have originated in the open sea. This action increases the fertility of areas like the Wadden Sea of the northern Netherlands, West Germany and Denmark. The Wadden Sea supports almost 60% of the North Sea's brown shrimp, more than 50% of the sole, 80% of the plaice and nearly all of the herring population in some part of their life cycle. The dock-side value of these species was nearly $110 million in 1983 [12].

Marine species dependent on US wetlands include menhaden, bluefish, sea trout, spot, mullet, croaker and striped bass. Shrimp, blue crabs, oysters and clams — all important economic shellfish — depend on coastal wetlands. Scientists have demonstrated a direct relationship between the existence and size of tidal wetlands and estuary and the production of a marine shrimp fishery [13]. Some shrimp species spend their entire life cycles in deep water; others spawn at sea, and then the larvae migrate to the coastal wetland nurseries where, together with the larvae of crabs and many fish such as milkfish (*Chanos chanos*), they grow quickly in the food-rich environment.

Mangroves support a wealth of fish, shellfish, prawns, oysters, clams and mussels. Mudskippers are cultivated in Taiwan as a great delicacy, and lassoed by children from elevated walkways in the coastal villages of southern Malaysia. The mudskippers feed on crabs and snails which in turn feed on decaying mangrove leaves or other vegetation. Snails range from the soil and sediment to roots and trunks where they may graze algae. Worms and microscopic plants and animals, all abundant in

Mark Boulton/ICCE

Fishing on Lake Ganvie, Benin. Coastal, lake and floodplain wetlands are productive spawning, nursery and feeding areas for fish. Nearly a third of the total African fish catch is thought to come from inland fisheries.

mangrove soil, process organic material, recycle nutrients and are food for higher animals. Mangrove fiddler crabs hatch their eggs to coincide with spring high tides each month, when the maximum flooding allows their larvae the best chance of survival [14].

Prawn species, such as tiger prawn and white prawn, depend on mangroves as food-rich nursery areas, and in turn support major tropical fisheries. Freshwater prawns (*Macrobrachium* spp.) spawn in the brackish waters of mangroves; the larvae feed in the estuary before migrating upstream to the freshwater environment. The mangrove crab (*Scylla serrata*) is now part of an important Indo-Pacific industry; they are fattened in special mangrove ponds in Taiwan, the Philippines, Singapore and Australia, and sold as a gourmet product.

Oysters are extensively harvested from among mangroves. Blood clams (*Anadara granosa*) and other cockles are extensively cultivated from the mudflats in front of Asian mangroves. Malaysia is the major producer, with 60,000 tonnes per year. Mussels are cultivated on mangrove or bamboo poles throughout southeast Asia, with yields of 250 tonnes per hectare possible. The cultivation and sale of all these species is possible on a village scale; this commerce can give sustained yields of major value while maintaining — indeed depending on — the natural ecological functions of the mangrove system.

Shrimp exports from developing to developed countries earn at least $900 million a year [15]. World exports of cod and herring are worth more than $580 million [16]. In 1980-81, wetland-dependent species earned New South Wales (Australia) $5.3 million, and oyster, scallop, crab and prawn a further $27 million. Mangroves in Thailand are estimated to be worth $130 per hectare per year in fisheries, compared to the gross income of $30 per hectare per year derived from using them for charcoal production [17].

In the Lower Mekong Basin, 236,000 tonnes out of a total fish catch of 500,000 tonnes per year is derived from wetlands. Thus in 1981 the wetlands directly contributed $90 million to the economy, as well as supplying 50-70% of the protein needs of the delta's 20 million people [18]. The rivers of the Mekong basin produce 60-92 kg of fish per hectare; the standing waters and seasonally flooded zones produce 198-291 kg/ha [19]. The river swamps of the US state of Georgia produce 239 kg/ha. Up to 80% of India's commercial fisheries in the Ganges-Brahmaputra estuary is based on the Sundarbans wetland complex.

While wetlands in developed nations produce large amounts of commercially valuable products, economic and nutritional dependence on wetlands is at its greatest among small Third World communities. About 1,000 people depend on the catch of freshwater shrimp from the Black River Lower Morass in Jamaica; for many it is the only source of income. The average annual catch for each fisherman is 400 kg, producing an income equivalent to $1,750 from shrimp alone.

Over 25,000 villagers around Lake Chilwa on the Malawi-Mozambique border rely on the rich fishery concentrated around the edge of the lake. Here, as with lake and floodplain rivers throughout the world, the annual migration and spawning of fish in the marginal wetlands depends totally on the flood cycle. Its success is vital to the survival of the fishing communities. More than 10,000 families in the inner delta of the Niger in northern Mali rely on an annual fish catch of 100,000 tonnes, worth $5 million.

Inland fisheries. Rivers and their floodplains produce about half of the world's inland fish catch of 10 million tonnes [20]. Many species may migrate short distances: the European carp on the floodplain of the Danube delta in Romania, the tilapia of the Okavango in Botswana, yellow perch, muskies and bass in Lake Michigan (US), and the largemouth bass in the shallow lakes of the southern United States. But others — salmon, trout, sunfish, pickerel and some carp — may all go considerable distances, some species moving upstream and others downstream [21].

Atlantic and Pacific salmon may migrate thousands of kilometres to spawning grounds in the aquatic vegetation beds of shallow river headwaters. Marine fish frequently move hundreds of kilometres up major rivers such as the Niger, the Mekong, the Magdalena of Colombia and the Murray River of south Australia [22]. Some species move long distances within single basins. Some fish in the Paraná River of South America swim 650-1,000 km — up to 16.7 km per day — in their reproductive cycles [23]. In the Niger, the characin fish *Alestes leuciscus* travelled up to 400 km before the construction of the Markala Dam [24]. The movement of species is often closely linked to the water cycles of the floodplains, so that fish arrive just as flooding starts. Thus spawning species moving up the Chari River from Lake Chad arrive at the Yaérés floodplains just as the waters begin to rise.

These migratory patterns underline three key points about wetland management.

* First, the benefits of wetlands may be felt at some considerable distance from their location; perhaps even in different countries.
* Second, such are the links between wetlands, rivers, lakes and the open sea that upsetting the water regime which normally maintains a wetland system and flooding cycle can have considerable knock-on effects.
* Third, the increasing regulation of water flow and development of floodplains for other land uses is increasingly devastating to natural fisheries.

Recreational fisheries. These are particularly important in the developed world where all freshwater recreational angling depends on wetlands. In the United States, almost half the saltwater catch is also associated with wetlands.

Fishing is the most popular 'sport' in the world. Its wetland component in the United States alone was worth $13 billion in the mid-1970s. At issue here is not only the enjoyment of the sportsmen but the financial spin-offs from recreational fishing in terms of equipment manufacturing and retail sales, licences, and income for resorts and tourism. Sport fishing is being identified by many coastal resorts in developing countries as an important potential source of foreign currency. A recent proposal for a national park in Jamaica's Negril Great Morass includes the creation of a lake partly for this purpose.

Aquaculture. Many species which depend on wetlands are being 'farmed', an activity which may require management, breeding and selection for increased production. These efforts involve such varied

*In Louisiana, combining crayfish farming and rice cultivation in the same
artificial ponds helps increase the profitability of wetland farming, and helps to
counter the unpredictability of markets. Such multiple cropping has much to offer
the Third World.*

species as carp, catfish, shrimp, crayfish, oysters, frogs, turtles,
alligators, crocodiles and duck.

Fish farming (pisciculture) has a long tradition in both Asia and
Europe, where fish such as carp have played an important part in diet,
festivities and social organisation. The state fisheries in Trebon
Biosphere Reserve, Czechoslovakia, annually produce about 2,000
tonnes of fish, 1,000 tonnes of duck and 100 tonnes of geese. Average
fish production from the 4,600 hectares of fishponds in this part of
Bohemia is 500 kg/ha. Recent trials with fertiliser and aeration of the
waters have produced yields of up to five tonnes per hectare in
experimental ponds, while results from Israel suggest that 'harvests' of
10 tonnes/hectare are possible.

Yields of crayfish (known locally as crawfish) from artificial ponds in
swampy southern Louisiana in the US can exceed 1.8 tonnes/hectare.
But the economic feasibility of such operations in nations with high
labour costs, like the United States, depends not on the food value of
the product but on market prices. Market prices in turn depend on the
size and timing of the harvest of crayfish in 'wild' wetlands, particularly
the Atchafalaya basin. In 1985, there was a bumper wild harvest, so the

profit margins for aquaculture farmers were poor; in some cases farmers lost money. When the price approaches $1.25 per kilo, however, the return on investment can be very attractive, and provide an economic incentive to put wetland — or to keep wetland — under water again.

By combining crayfish farming and rice cultivation in the same pond, flooding of the pond in autumn allows the recently hatched crayfish to feed on the rice stubble. They reach market size by December or January, and harvesting can continue into the spring. The new rice crop can then be sown. As the pond slowly drains, the remaining adult crayfish, supplemented with additional stock for breeding, burrow deep into the soil until the pond is again flooded. The rice crop can then be harvested without damaging the breeding population. In 1984, an experimental scheme was begun in Louisiana combining cypress plantation with crayfish production.

This type of multiple cropping system has much to offer countries in Africa, Asia and Latin America for raising protein and timber in their wetlands, as well as selling expensive crayfish meat to the gourmet markets of the developed world. The particular appeal of this timber/aquaculture system is that it at least partially reestablishes the basic wetland ecological 'services' and landscape.

Developing nations are becoming interested in aquaculture not only as a domestic economic enterprise but particularly as an earner of foreign currency. Indonesia exported 26,000 tonnes of shrimp in 1983, earning $190 million. In 1984 the Indonesian minister of agriculture, Achmad Affandi, predicted an increase in annual output to 44,700 tonnes, worth $530 million. The country has the potential to establish 700,000 hectares of ponds for shrimp breeding, and to increase the present harvest a hundredfold: from 0.1-0.6 tonnes per hectare to the 10-12 tonnes per hectare attained in Taiwan [25].

In Thailand, cockles, oysters and mussels produce 24, 90 and 180 tonnes per year respectively. Fish ponds in the Philippines with an annual yield of three tonnes per hectare generate an income of $1,782 per hectare per year [26].

The use of floating net cages as fish rearing pens is becoming more common in coastal wetlands such as the mangrove fringes of southern Malaysia and the Seto Inland Sea of Japan. In Japan, cages 6x6x4 metres stocked with yellow-tail *Seriola quinquiradiata* yield 1.5-2.5 tonnes per cage after 7-8 months [27]. Proposals for the development of aquaculture in Jamaican wetlands forecast shrimp production of 2.84 tonnes per hectare [28] which could generate an income of over US$10,000 for a family operating a 2.6 hectare pond system.

A recent study of the economic potential of Jamaica's Negril and Black River Lower Morasses by two Swedish researchers [29] proposes an integrated aquaculture system involving shrimp, tilapia, duck and crocodile, which would yield shrimp, fish fillet, dressed duck, crocodile meat and crocodile skin. The fish and duck combination makes optimum use of the volume of water. The duck droppings fertilise the ponds, and there is a reduced parasite and disease problem in both populations. Offal from the processing industry can be used to supplement the feed for the crocodiles.

Crocodile and alligator skins were worth over $50 per metre of animal in 1977, while the meat could earn another $70 per animal. About 15,000 are killed commercially each year in Louisiana and Florida in controlled hunts. The meat has become a gourmet delicacy in some of the South's more famous ethnic restaurants. Uncontrolled hunting in the late 19th Century and rapidly inflating prices in the 20th Century (prices increasing fiftyfold between 1916 and 1963) caused the virtual extinction of the alligator in parts of the South. Alligators were strictly protected in the 1960s and 1970s, and alligator farming projects are now on the increase in the southern United States.

In Zimbabwe and Zambia there are farms producing Nile crocodile. In Latin America, southeast Asia and Australia there are projects for caiman production; the animals are highly productive and grow rapidly. A proposal to establish a crocodile farm in Jamaica estimates that the initial investment of US$125,000 would be repaid in four years and profit would then be derived from an annual production of 600 animals.

Proceed with caution. The above figures on the protein production of aquaculture in wetlands are impressive, and encouraging to those who want to use wetlands for such activities. But there are other considerations which need to be taken into account before starting such programmes.

The average yearly animal protein production in swamps and marshes is nine grammes per square metre, which is 3.5 times the average for natural terrestrial ecosystems. Estuaries are twice as productive again as swamps and marshes [30]. The protein yield from fish dependent on mangroves is greater than that derived from the cultivation of crops (including rice) in the converted wetland. But this yield is usually not visible to 'developers' and would-be developers.

Even the high yields of various types of aquaculture may not be as high as those of the area of wetland which the 'fish farm' (or alligator farm) replaced. The development of aquaculture exacts an environmental and ecological cost. Several wetland scientists, such as Eugene Turner at the Center for Wetland Resources, Louisiana State University, and Armando de la Cruz at Mississippi State University, question the wisdom of converting coastal wetlands to aquaculture without doing the profit-loss equations very carefully. Natural, undisturbed fisheries, along with the other support systems of wetlands, are provided without energy inputs and at no environmental cost. Wild wetland might often prove more productive than altered, managed wetland.

In many tropical countries, such as the Philippines, mangroves are rapidly making way for fish farms. Dr de la Cruz is one of many scientists expressing concern over the effects of clear cutting mangroves to make way for "the quick economic return and lucrative economic benefits of aquaculture" [31]. Loss of the shoreline mangroves destroys the nurseries of economically important fish such as milkfish (*Chanos chanos*) and of shrimp, both of which which are actually used to stock the new aquaculture ponds. Along the southern coast of Luzon, hundreds of local people derive a living from collecting shrimp and milkfish fry for ponds [32]. De la Cruz maintains that "conversion of mangrove areas into fish ponds, rice paddies or any other form of land use that will remove the vegetation, alter water circulation patterns, increase sedimentation, or introduce harmful biological or non-biological pollutants into the mangrove estuary will definitely affect the ecological functions of mangroves as a whole".

The work in Louisiana, however, suggests that there may be ways of maintaining the basic ecological integrity and functions of the important mangrove ecosystems, while producing fish and crustaceans for market at the same time. But success will not come from separating ecological and financial functions — as is being done in the Philippines — but from combining them, as is being tried in Louisiana. Over half the mangrove lands in the Philippines are already devoted to aquaculture. A recent survey in Bangladesh found that more than 95% of its 628,780 hectares of mangroves are suitable for aquaculture [33]. The financial lures of aquaculture must be moderated by economic forecasts which go beyond reckoning the profits of individual fish farms, and accurately cost the loss of the entire ecosystem.

Animals for fur

Questions of cruelty and animal rights aside, wetlands produce many of the world's valuable furs. Some 85% of the pelts harvested in Louisiana in 1976-77 were from wetlands, and the state's wetlands contribute 40-65% of the entire US fur harvest. The total value of all sales was $24 million; the main species were coypu (which produces the fur nutria), muskrat, raccoon, mink and river otter. Trapping provides extra income and off-season employment to farm workers and fishermen. At its height the state industry employed 20,000 people, but today the figure is closer to 6,000. Early this century, three million muskrat (*Ondatra zibethicus rivalicus*) were caught in a single season. Since its accidental introduction in 1938, the Argentinian coypu (*Myocaster coypus*) has dominated the harvest. Since then over 100 million have been trapped on the marshlands and in the swamps. Muskrat, however, can be so prolific that nearly 50 animals per hectare can be caught annually.

Obviously the harvest of these and other animals must be coordinated carefully with efforts by conservationists and governments to protect these animals in the wild, and with the regulations laid down by international treaties controlling trade in such products.

Chapter 2

What are wetlands?

Wetland is a collective term for ecosystems whose formation has been dominated by water, and whose processes and characteristics are largely controlled by water. A wetland is a place that has been wet enough for a long enough time to develop specially adapted vegetation and other organisms.

The US Corps of Engineers defines wetlands as "those areas that are inundated or saturated by surface or groundwater at a frequency and duration sufficient to support, and that under normal circumstances do support, a prevalence of vegetation typically adapted for life in saturated soil conditions. Wetlands generally include swamps, marshes, bogs and similar areas."

The 1971 Ramsar convention on wetlands of international importance defines them as "areas of marsh, fen, peatland or water, whether natural or artificial, permanent or temporary, with water that is static or flowing, fresh, brackish or salt, including areas of marine water the depth of which at low tide does not exceed six metres". Many such areas form peat, the partly decomposed remains of surface vegetation, which becomes deeper as litter accumulates. In Europe, peat-forming systems are usually collectively known as 'mires', though this term is also used to describe many other types of wetland. Others simply call wet peat areas 'bogs'.

The problem of defining 'wetland' is important not only to the lexicographer and geographer; in the United States, it has become a major legal and financial issue. Both the public and scientists are becoming increasingly concerned about the rate at which US wetlands are disappearing; some 54% have been lost since the Europeans arrived on the continent, with saltmarshes still disappearing at a rate approaching 1% annually.

Federal and state laws are exerting more and more control over activities in wetlands. In May 1977 President Carter issued Executive Order No. 11990 — 'Protection of Wetlands' — which made wetland conservation a priority for all federal agencies, and provided funds for the purpose. The Clean Water Act of 1977 established new standards for dredge and fill activities and stiffer controls over activities affecting wetlands. It authorised a $6 million 'National Wetland Inventory', authorised the Environmental Protection Agency to help states enforce controls, and required better evaluation of wetland impacts. Most coastal states (and many inland states) have adopted wetland protection acts or written regulations into laws relating to shoreland or floodplains. Court actions have emphasised US concern. In 1972, the US Court of Appeals ruled that the Army Corps of Engineers had the right to refuse a permit for filling in an area of mangroves in Florida. Since a court case in 1975, wetlands have been legally included in the definition of 'waters of the United States', so that activities in them — such as dredging and filling — require a Corps of Engineers permit.

In 1981 a group of hunters and fishermen called the Avoyelles Sportsman's League brought a case against a farming development in Louisiana when the landowners began to drain bottomland hardwood forest on their own property. The case established that such considerations as frequency of flooding, soil type and vegetation were acceptable criteria for defining wetlands. The court ordered the 8,000 hectare draining and clearing operation to stop, in a ruling which became a landmark in wetland protection.

The US Fish and Wildlife Service is currently working on a National Wetland Inventory that is producing maps of diverse wetland types throughout the country. Several wetland research institutes — at Baton Rouge (Louisiana), Gainesville (Florida) and Savannah (Georgia) — have been established, reflecting the degree of interest in and concern for these ecosystems.

How wetlands are formed

Compared with other major natural forms of landscape, wetlands are young and dynamic. Many are physically unstable, changing in a season or even in a single storm. They change as vegetation changes, sediments are laid down or land sinks. The processes which formed some wetlands stopped long ago, so they may be regarded as fossil landscapes. In other cases, a single, recent event initiated them. A major flood in 1973 created the first islands of the Atchafalaya delta, the newest of the Mississippi delta complex.

Man has been a major factor in wetland formation since prehistoric times. In Britain, forest clearance in the uplands helped trigger soil and vegetation changes, which altered hydrology and led in some places to bog formation. More recently, the flooding of peat diggings excavated in the Middle Ages to satisfy the fuel needs of local communities created the shallow lakes, marginal fens and marshes which make up the Norfolk Broads of eastern England. Reservoirs, canals, ditches, flooded gravel pits, and the extensive fish ponds of Bohemia, many created by medieval feudal landlords, are all examples of man-made wetlands.

During the last glacial period in the Northern Hemisphere, which ended about 10,000 years ago, ice carved out depressions in bedrock, leaving shallow lakes throughout many high latitude countries, especially Canada and Scandinavia. As the ice retreated, large blocks were often left stranded on plains where sediment continued to accumulate. When the ice finally melted, it left a hollow which became flooded or seasonally waterlogged. The famous prairie potholes of the United States and Canada, so important for duck populations, formed in this way.

The Pleistocene ice ages (2 million-10,000 years ago) disrupted drainage patterns and trapped water in lakes formed in front of ice sheets and glaciers, such as Lake Pickering in northern England. The 'lake' in fact no longer exists; its last remnants were drained for agriculture by Cistercian monks and farmers in the Middle Ages. In many such areas, open water no longer exists, but vestiges of marshland remain on periodically flooded former lake beds.

In the Arctic, after the upper layer of frozen soil melts in the summer, the water is often unable to drain because of the impermeable permafrost (permanently frozen ground) below. Where there is no permafrost, waterlogging may still persist through much of the summer because of low slope angles, low evaporation rates, sudden releases of water from melting snow, or high water storage in peat. Bogs, fens, marsh, peatlands and — south of the tree line — swamps abound in the Arctic. Collectively, this peaty wetland complex is often called 'muskeg'.

On the Arctic coastal plain, thaw lakes are produced during the summer melt and tend to advance by erosion in the direction of the prevailing wind. Other lakes are formed in depressions formed by ice wedges, collapsed pingos (blisters of ice), or increasingly through surface changes caused by human activities. Any surface change (e.g. erosion, damage to vegetation, or construction) which alters the thermal balance increases summer melting and the formation of open water. The tracks of seismic survey vehicles which searched for oil during the 1960s are still visible in Alaska as parallel channels of open water. Depressions have also been left by the building of the Trans-Alaska Pipeline.

Sea level change. Much coastal wetland formation or destruction is controlled by the dynamics and balance of sea level movement. Sea level has generally been rising since the last major advances of glaciers in the Pleistocene, when enormous quantities of water were locked up on land as ice. Recent rises in sea level have led to the accumulation of up to 16 metres of peat in the coastal marshes of Jamaica, and favoured the development of extensive saltmarshes on the gently sloping eastern coast of the United States, and of marshes and fens in the Fenlands and the Somerset Levels of England, the pocosin (a name derived from an Algonquin Indian word meaning 'swamp-on-a-hill' — see Chapter 4) swamps of the US Carolinas and the extensive coastal peatlands of Hokkaido, Japan.

Environments protected from waves by reefs, barrier islands and harbours, and those with gently sloping coastal lowlands, favour wetland development.

By contrast, where land is rising in comparison with the sea, as on parts of the South Island of New Zealand where the fiord coastline produced by former glaciations is very steep, coastal marshes do not readily form. New Zealand is rising due to the movement of the tectonic plate it occupies. Land areas depressed by massive weights of ice, such as Scotland, all of Scandinavia and parts of Canada, have been rising since removal of the ice. In the Mississippi delta, which is sinking because of the deformation of the crust under the weight of the sediment, marshes are being lost to natural subsidence and erosion.

Climate. The extensive bogs which typify the wetlands of Ireland, western Britain and southwest Norway are produced because more rain falls than evaporates in these oceanic climates. This favours the development of acidic and waterlogged conditions low in oxygen — ideal for the accumulation of peat. Only plants tolerant of acidic, waterlogged and nutrient-deficient conditions survive, e.g. *Sphagnum* bog mosses and Cotton grass (*Eriophorum* spp.). As rainfall declines eastward in Europe, the bogs are able to support trees, such as the mountain pine *Pinus montana* in Switzerland. Similar forested bogs are found throughout Canada and the northern United States.

High rainfall in mountain areas promotes wetland formation despite the fact that the land around the mountains may be relatively dry. Examples include the fens and bogs of Kosciusko National Park in the Snowy Mountains of Australia, the upland peats of Tasmania, the bogs on the side of Mount Kenya, and Ozegehara Bog on Honshu, Japan. Some researchers believe that many Western European bogs — especially raised and blanket bogs (see below) — are no longer active, having been initiated and developed in a wetter and cooler era than the present.

The lay of the land. Any process which produces a hollow or depression in the landscape may produce a wetland. They can even occur in deserts, provided the depressions collect water from a wide enough catchment area. Where springs or groundwater supplies are adequate, substantial wetlands can form in other dry surroundings, e.g. the deep peats of the Bega Swamp and other peatlands on the Southern Tablelands of New South Wales, Australia, an environment elsewhere dominated by dry grasslands and eucalyptus forest.

Animals and events. Animal activity can produce and alter wetland habitats. Beavers do it through damming rivers and streams. In some of the forested areas of North America, there are beaver dams more than

500 years old. Unpredictable landscape processes can also produce wetlands. Faulting led to the development of marshes in San Francisco Bay; lava flow blocked drainage at Ozegehara and produced arguably the most famous and certainly the most visited bog in Japan; landslips on steep valley sides of the North Yorkshire Moors of Britain have created hollows in which bogs have developed.

Wetland dynamics

Wetlands — particularly mires — provide classic examples of 'ecological succession', where a plant community alters environmental conditions in a way that makes the habitat less favourable for its own survival but more favourable for the development of a different community. Wetland ecosystems can pass through many such stages, emphasising their dynamic yet ephemeral nature.

Aquatic plants, such as water lily or duckweed, may be the first higher plants to colonise the open water of a shallow pond. These produce organic detritus which adds to other sediments, and the pond gradually fills. As the water becomes shallower, emergent plants (plants growing up out of the water) such as rushes, sedges, reeds and grasses can establish and eventually shade out the aquatics. The pond becomes a marsh.

If organic debris builds up fast enough to accumulate peat, and the depression receives nutrient-rich groundwater or runoff, a fen may form. If the site relies on precipitation for water, the marsh may change instead to a bog.

Fens can also become bogs as peat builds up and the surface becomes more remote from the influence of groundwater. The bog may expand beyond the original confines of the pond basin and become a blanket bog. Eventually the bog may outgrow its ability to maintain a permanently high water table; trees then become established, if human activities and climate allow. This might also occur after the marsh or fen stage, producing carr (see Chapter 3) woodland, fen carr and eventually climax woodland — depending on hydrological conditions and management.

Wetlands throughout the world have gone through similar successional changes. The base of pocosin peats (evergreen shrub-scrub bogs) in North Carolina is dominated by marsh deposits, and in some cases by the remains of trees — such as Atlantic white cedar and cypress forest — indicating major changes in wetland type. Mangrove and saltmarshes 'build' land, making the environment less suitable for pioneering mangrove and more suitable for other, succeeding species. As the mangrove moves seawards in New Guinea, it is replaced by nipa swamp forest, which is more competitive in the increasingly fresh water. Saltmarshes can evolve into marshes dominated by grass or rush, then into reedswamp, followed by progressive drying, followed by carr and finally full woodland. Deltas and other floodplain areas similarly change and evolve over time as channels shift and areas are flooded regularly or starved of sediment.

Many in one

One wetland is often many different wetlands. Plant and animal species change according to the depth, duration and volume of flooding, lay of the land and soil types.

The Shire River Elephant Marshes in Malawi have a pattern common to the floodplains of the tropics and subtropics. In the deep water zone there are aquatic plants and floating islands of plants. The 'swamp zone', with water 50-200 cm deep, has floating meadows and standing vegetation. The 'marsh zone' (20-100 cm deep) is dominated by the sedge *Cyperus digitatus*, with occasional floating plants. Outward from this are the grasslands, dominated by water-tolerant species.

Coastal floodplains or deltas are even more diverse because of the complexities of the salt and fresh water mixing. This provides habitat favourable for wildlife, but makes management much more difficult. The coastal marshes of the Ganges-Brahmaputra delta support the dense brackish-water forests known as the Sundarbans. Behind the protective screen of coastal mangroves lies a complex of different floodplain zones, differentiated by variations in flooding pattern and vegetation. In the Mississippi delta of Louisiana, zones follow salinity: saltmarsh plants dominate the saline coastal zone; more and different species appear as the water becomes fresher with increasing distance from the sea. The timbered wetlands begin in the zones unaffected by salt water.

Chapter 3

Types of wetland I:
Marshes, swamps and mires

Part of the confusion about what wetlands are can be put down to confusion over what they are called. Because their study falls under no single science, because they occur all over the world in every climate, and because of their strong association with the lives of the earliest humans, the same kind of wetlands in different countries can be known by different names. For example, a billabong in Australia is known as a lagoon, 'cut-off' or backswamp elsewhere. North Americans define 'swamps' as wetlands dominated by trees or shrubs, which are flooded through all or most of the growing season. In Britain and Europe, such wetlands are called 'carr' and are characterised by alder and willows. Sometimes they develop in association with peat deposits in valley bottoms and produce a distinctive 'fen-carr' landscape.

In Europe, place names often reflect the language of wetland landscapes, revealing the nature of the terrain at the time of settlement. The village of Marske in northeast England derives its name from the Old English 'mersc' (marsh); more obvious links are evident in towns like Crakemarsh and Tidmarsh. Kerr, a Middle English derivative from the Old Norse 'Kjarr', was used in England in the Middle Ages (13th-16th Century) — according to Margaret Gelling, a leading authority on English place names — to describe "a marsh, especially one overgrown by brushwood". The word has since become 'carr'.

'Mire' derives from the Old Norse 'myrr', and is generally used to describe all peat-forming wetlands. The Old English 'sloh' (slough), meaning a watercourse running in a hollow, is not only reflected in the names of English towns like Slough, but has entered the wetland terminology of North America to describe the channels feeding the Everglades and smaller features throughout the United States.

Marsh

Marshes vary greatly, depending on their origin, geographical location, water regimes, chemistry and soil or sediment characteristics. They are dominated by herbaceous plants and sustained by water sources other than direct rainfall. They are among the most productive ecosystems in

Simon Warner/WWF

Reedbeds on the edge of a saltmarsh near Titchwell in Norfolk, UK. Among the most productive ecosystems in the world, marshes are a vital link between land and water, sustaining important fisheries and protecting the land's edge from erosion.

the world. A vital link between terrestrial and aquatic environments, they sustain important fisheries and protect the land's edge from erosion.

There are three major groups of marsh:

* *Tidal saltmarshes* are typical of temperate shorelines between high and low tidal extremes. They dominate large areas of the eastern coast of North America and coastal Europe, and are generally dissected by a complex of tidal creeks, important conduits for sediment, nutrients and organic matter.

  Saltmarshes are most common in sheltered coastal zones rich in marine sediment. Examples include Chesapeake Bay in Maryland, Hudson Bay in Canada, and the areas behind the spits, bars and offshore islands of the eastern coast of North America, Western Europe and the Mediterranean. They are also found inland, even as far from the sea as the landlocked US states of Utah and the Dakotas, where evaporation and drainage basins make for very salty soil.

* *Tidal freshwater marshes* are found further inland than saltmarshes, at the head of tides. They are affected by tidal cycles

Edward Maltby

The Florida Everglades of the southeastern United States is one of the world's biggest marshes. Aquatic plants dominate areas of open water, together with floating mats of 'periphyton' (complex associations of algae and diatoms).

but not exposed to salt water stress. They support a more diverse plant life than their saltmarsh counterparts, producing for example the vivid seasonal changes in colour of the Maryland marshes.

* *Freshwater marshes* are dominated by grasses and sedges but are very different in origin and appearance. They account for over 90% of the wetland area in the United States (excluding Alaska and Hawaii), but are prominent in all latitudes where groundwater, surface springs, streams or runoff causes frequent flooding or more or less permanent shallow water flooding.

Water flowing into marshes (which may be surface runoff, groundwater or tidal flow), and the expansion and contraction of marshes, supplies the marsh system with nutrients. This distinguishes them sharply from 'bogs', which are essentially rainfed and low in nutrients.

By the European definition, inland 'marshes' occur on mineral soils and do not accumulate peat. 'Fens' are peat-forming freshwater wetlands, generally non-acidic, receiving nutrients mainly from groundwater sources, and dominated by marsh-like vegetation. Where

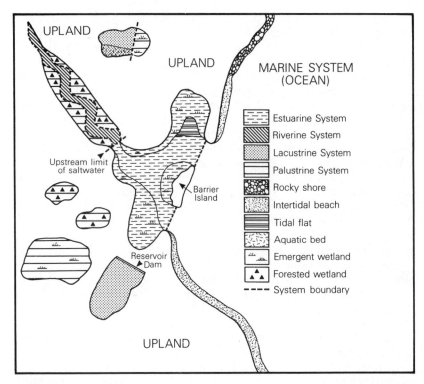

UPLAND

UPLAND

MARINE SYSTEM
(OCEAN)

Upstream limit
of saltwater

Barrier
Island

Reservoir
Dam

UPLAND

Estuarine System

Riverine System

Lacustrine System

Palustrine System

Rocky shore

Intertidal beach

Tidal flat

Aquatic bed

Emergent wetland

Forested wetland

System boundary

Major US wetland types.

reeds dominate but the soil is not necessarily peaty, the term 'reedswamp' is commonly used. To confuse things further, the extensive tracts of peatland on Hokkaido in Japan, the fenlands of Britain and many tropical lowlands are dominated by reeds, and so can be called reedswamp. But if the reedswamp supports peat, it may be called a fen. In the tropics, wetlands dominated by papyrus (*Cyperus papyrus*) and cattail (*Typha*) are generally called 'swamps'.

North Americans make no verbal distinction according to whether or not the wetland forms peat. In the most recent classification by the US Fish and Wildlife Service, marshes are described as persistent or non-persistent emergent wetlands and classified according to whether they are associated with rivers, lakes or other waterlogged land [34].

Marshes are commonly found in the wettest areas of floodplains and around the fringes of permanent water bodies, from the smallest ponds to the largest lakes. One of the world's biggest marshes is in the Florida

Everglades, which once covered over 10,000 sq km from Lake Okeechobee to the southwest tip of Florida. The flat, low limestone surface slopes southwards at less than 3 cm per kilometre. Natural drainage water flows at only a kilometre a day.

The total dominance of sawgrass *Cladium jamaicense* (hence the description "River of Grass") over large areas of the Everglades which have escaped drainage and development actually conceals a greater variety of wetland types and more complex communities. Under optimal conditions the sawgrass forms a monoculture, with plants up to three metres high. But the plant also grows with cattail, rushes, maidencane grass and herbs. Aquatic plants dominate areas of open water, together with floating mats of periphyton (complex associations of algae and diatoms). Various islands of trees interrupt the continuity of the sawgrass marsh. Recent invasions of three exotic species — Australian pine (*Casuarina* spp.), Brazilian pepper (*Schinus terebinthifolius*) and cajeput (*Melaleuca quinquenervia*) — have raised concern for the future of the ecological character of the Everglades.

The summer flooding pattern of the world's largest sawgrass marsh, now protected within the half million hectares of the Everglades National Park, is no longer natural. It is controlled by the South Florida Water Management District and the US Corps of Engineers, a process of alteration which began in 1881 with the first drainage and canal projects. Ironically, the threats to sawgrass marsh and associated wetlands come not only from the changes in water regime induced by settlement and development. The sawgrass glades, wet prairies and saltmarshes need periodic fires; without them, sawgrass communities accumulate too much litter and are replaced by other species [35].

Historically, fires started by lightening have been common, but only in the wet season, when plant roots and underlying peat are protected. But first the Indians and then the waves of white colonists reaching south Florida at the turn of the century set dry season fires, which have drastically reduced the sawgrass marsh. Dry season fires are now more likely to be severe, to consume the peat soil and completely destroy the flammable vegetation. Sawgrass has been replaced by other species (including willow) over large areas, and in some areas by bare rock, largely because of deliberate fires and poor water controls. As early as 1952 the US ecologist F.E. Egler argued that "the herbaceous everglade and surrounding pinelands were born in fires; ... they can survive only with fires; ... they are dying today because of fires" [36].

We are still learning about the role of fire in maintaining certain wetlands (especially marshes). The lessons learned in the Everglades may have much to teach us about the sound management of marshes and swamps throughout the world.

Edward Maltby

The cypress swamps of the southern United States are attractive but forbidding places. Green layers of duckweed often conceal mosquitoes and poisonous snakes. But the swamps also support a wealth of animal and plant life.

Swamps

Swamps develop in still water areas, around lake margins, and in parts of floodplains such as sloughs or oxbows (cut-off remnants of bends in rivers) — often described as 'backswamps'. The cypress swamps of the southern states are among the most attractive yet forbidding places. Mosquitoes and such poisonous snakes as the cottonmouth mocassin are often concealed by the green layer of duckweed, and are natural deterrents to all but the most determined human visitors. Alligators, tree frogs, the introduced coypu and many varieties of heron are frequently visible parts of a rich and diverse wildlife.

The character of wooded wetlands varies according to geographic location and environment. In the northern United States, red maple, ash, northern white cedar, black spruce and larch are prominent; in the south, bald cypress, water tupelo, black gums, Atlantic white cedar, oaks and willows dominate.

In New Guinea, the swamp forests dominated by *Melaleuca* trees are flooded to 1.5 metres or more in the wet season. Palms such as sago palm and *Pandanus* species are a common understory. In dense stands

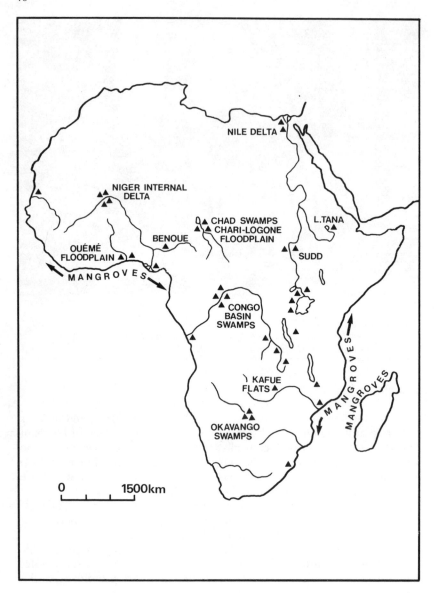

The principal swamps of Africa.

the fronds of the palm can produce a completely closed canopy, always dark and without undergrowth — the opposite of the cypress swamps of Louisiana. Lush groves occupy river bottomlands, lake margins, creeks and pools. Because Papuans have traditionally relied on sago flour as a staple food, they dam up watercourses to create swamps in which the palm thrives [37].

The flora of the wetlands (the swamp) is far more important in almost every way than that of the hillside undergrowth of the rainforest, argues one wetland expert. "As a source of produce requiring no kind of care, the swamp is a 'mudmine' of lasting merit" [38]. The American Indians of the Amazon-Orinoco regions similarly developed a palm food culture based on moriche (*Mauritia flexuosa*).

The swamp palm forests of the Caribbean have dwindled rapidly, so the swamp forests of equatorial southeast Asia, the Pacific and the Amazon represent some of the largest remaining forest reserves. Very little of these forests has been inventoried. More than a quarter of Indonesia is swamp; in Sumatra the proportion is 30%, and Kalimantan supports nearly 20 million hectares of swamp, more than half with peaty soils. The Riau swamp of Sumatra covers over a million hectares, and the swampland between the Huntschein Range and the Sepik estuary in Papua New Guinea covers 620,000 hectares [39]. We have no idea how extensive are the swamps of Irian Jaya.

Herbaceous swamps

Reedswamps are the most productive ecological systems on earth. They are dominated by the reed species *Phragmites australis* in North America, Europe, Australasia and parts of South America. The tropical papyrus *Cyperus papyrus* is often considered more characteristic of African swamps, but *Typha* species (e.g. *Typha domingensis*) are also common.

Most reedswamps fringe wetlands of the sort once common on the edge of European lakes and river floodplains. Reeds provide excellent habitats for waterfowl, birds (e.g. the reed and great reed warblers) and aquatic animals.

The area of reedswamp worldwide has fallen as shallow, open water has been drained. In Europe, reedswamp is also being lost to so-called 'reed-death', where inflowing drainage water enriched with fertiliser increases nutrient content in the lakes. The reeds grow faster but produce weaker stems. They are then far more susceptible to physical damage. In the Norfolk Broads of England, physical damage has increased with the dramatic increase in recreational boating and fishing in recent years. Reed-death has also come to the Swiss midlands, between the Jurassic and Alpine mountains. This is the most densely

Mark Boulton/ICCE

settled part of Switzerland, an overcultivated area where the last wetland remnants are squeezed between highly developed land. Reed-death can reduce wetland fringes at a rate of 1-3 metres a year. Less than 10% of the original reedbed in the Swiss midlands has survived [40].

The form of many large tropical African lakes — Chad, Bangweulu (Zambia), Mweru (Zaire/Zambia), Upemba (Zaire), George (Uganda), Naivasha (Kenya), Malombe (Malawi) and Chilwa (Malawi/Mozambique) — favours marginal swamp development. Indeed, there may be more swamp than open water in tropical Africa [41].

Marginal swamps play a vital role in the life cycle of aquatic organisms, and sustain rich fisheries and abundant wildlife. Like saltmarshes, they have different vegetation zones, usually in response to variations in water depth and nutrient levels. Papyrus dominates most of these swamps. At Lake Chilwa on the Malawi/Mozambique border, *Typha* is the major species. The high salt and alkaline levels of the Lake Chilwa sediments give *Typha* a competitive advantage over the papyrus, which is restricted to more acidic zones of the lake area. As problems of salinisation and reduced water quality increase throughout tropical

Mangrove forests like these on the Kenyan coast (left) provide storm protection, support for the marine food web, nurseries for valuable fish and crustaceans, and habitat for plants and animals. But mangroves are concentrated in some of the world's poorest countries. The bleak expanse above is all that remains of a mangrove forest in Haiti cleared by peasants for wood to make charcoal.

Africa, it seems inevitable that the highly valued resources of the papyrus swamps are likely to decline and be replaced by other less useful plants, such as *Typha*.

Mangrove swamps

Mangrove swamps are the sub-tropical and tropical equivalents of the temperate saltmarsh. Most are limited to within 25° North and South of the Equator, but they can reach higher latitudes (up to about 32° in the Northern Hemisphere) where local conditions limit frosts to less than five consecutive days. Mangroves (conservationists have recently taken to referring to them as 'forests' to avoid the pejorative word 'swamp') cover at least 14 million hectares and are concentrated in some of the world's poorest nations.

Broadly, they are forests which tolerate salt and occupy the intertidal zone. They constitute a reservoir and refuge for many unusual plants and animals; about 60 species of mangrove tree and shrub, and over

2,000 species of fish, invertebrates and epiphytic plants (plants that grow on other plants, but are not parasitic) depend on mangroves for survival.

They have also played an important part in the economies of tropical peoples for thousands of years, providing a wide range of timber products and other materials on a sustainable basis. But the values of the indirect functions of mangrove swamps are at least comparable, if not greater: environmental and storm protection; support for the marine food web through food supply and nursery functions for many species, including commercially important fish, shrimp and crab stocks; habitat for a wide range of animals and plants with harvestable products such as wax and honey; aesthetic and recreational value; and scientific importance as a genetic resource.

They are extremely varied. Giant closed forests of red mangrove and black mangrove grow 40-50 metres high in parts of Brazil, Colombia, Ecuador and Venezuela. In Asia and Oceania the richer flora of the Old World forms the familiar tangled and almost impenetrable closed forests. On more arid coasts and near the extremes of their climatic range (such as in Florida, Louisiana and the Japanese Pacific islands) stunted shrubs less than a metre high form open communities, often with discrete and widely separated clumps.

The greatest concentration of mangroves is in the Indian Ocean-West Pacific region; about a fifth of the world's mangroves border the sheltered Sunda Shelf region enclosed by Vietnam, Thailand, Malaysia, Sumatra, Java and Borneo. Nearly 10 million hectares extend from the east coast of tropical Africa to eastern Australia and New Zealand. The Niger delta has a further 700,000 hectares of mangrove. The largest remaining contiguous area is the Sundarbans forest, covering nearly a million hectares of the Ganges delta [42].

Mangrove forests too have their sub-zones, with red mangroves — frequently regarded as pioneers — growing in the continually flooded zone below low water. These give way to the often taller black mangroves towards the high tide level. Once established, the network of horizontal or 'cable' roots, which anchor the trees to the soft mud, trap more sediment. This enables mangrove 'pioneers' to move progressively seawards, accelerates shore development and ensures coastal stability.

The march of mangroves towards the sea can exceed 100 metres a year. Palenbang, a thriving port on the north coast of Sumatra when visited by Marco Polo in the 13th Century, is today 50 kilometres inland [43]. The government of Bangladesh, anxious to stabilise the highly mobile, new, but often temporary islands in the Bay of Bengal, is planting mangroves as one means of achieving this. The resulting buildup of land helps agricultural expansion, but such gains are forfeited if farmers then clear the mangroves to get land. This clearing destroys

Type of resource or product	Location	Date	Value (US$/ha/year)
Complete mangrove ecosystem	Trinidad Fiji Puerto Rico	1974 1976 1973	500 950-1,250 1,550
Forestry products	Trinidad Indonesia Malaysia Thailand	1974 1978 1980 1982	70 10-20 25 30-400
Fishery products	Trinidad Indonesia Fiji Queensland Thailand	1974 1978 1976 1976 1982	125 50 640 1,975 30-100 (fish) 200-2,000 (shrimp)
Recreation, tourism	Trinidad	1974	200

Examples of economic values placed on mangrove systems and mangrove ecosystem products. Source: Hamilton and Snedaker 1984.

the natural protection afforded by mangroves against the storm surges of the frequent cyclones of the region.

Mangroves often extend considerable distances up tidal creeks. These may appear to be freshwater, but in fact denser salt water often forms a saline wedge far inland under the freshwater river flow. The mangrove roots grow at a level at least periodically washed by the salt wedge. This extends several kilometres up the Black River in Jamaica. Behind the mangrove fringe in New Guinea there are extensive tracts of Nipa forest (*Nypa fructicans*). The dense root growth of the palm is also important in stabilising the unconsolidated sediment of estuaries after initial colonisation by mangrove.

The whole ecological complex of the mangrove is often referred to as 'mangal'. The organic debris produced by the vegetation, together with shelter it provides and local environmental conditions, promotes food chain support and spawning and nursery conditions for many invertebrates and fish of major economic value, such as milkfish, mullet, groupers and snappers. As much as 80% of the Indian fishery catch from the lower delta region of the Ganges/Brahmaputra comes from the Sundarbans [44]; numerous timber products from the region underline the more direct commercial value of the mangroves.

The future of mangroves looks increasingly uncertain, given their

Mangrove timber in the Sundarbans, Bangladesh. Mangroves have helped to support tropical economies for thousands of years. But more and more are being cut on a shorter rotation, reducing their natural diversity.

conversion to other uses and the overexploitation of their natural products.

* In southeast Asia, conversion to rice paddies and aquaculture is occurring at an unprecedented rate [45], and oil spillages have resulted in large losses. During the Vietnam war, 40,000 hectares near Saigon were destroyed by herbicides; 15 years on, there was little evidence of recovery [46]. Between 1967 and 1975, an annual loss of 24,000 hectares was reported from the Philippines. At least 5,000 hectares per year are lost in the production of wood chips in Malaysia, and Thailand has lost up to 20% of its mangrove cover in the past decade [47].

* Only 25% of the original mangrove area of 24,300 hectares is left in Puerto Rico, and in Trinidad the government plans to develop large areas for agriculture and industry. Haiti and other West Indian islands have already lost large areas of mangrove.

* The exploitable age of trees in the Sundarbans has been estimated at 50-160 years, but more and more areas are being cut on a shorter rotation. As plantation forestry increases, the natural

diversity and ecological quality of the original mangrove forest will decline. As a response, three sanctuaries covering 32,000 hectares have been set up in the Bangladesh Sundarbans, mainly to protect tigers and other wildlife. Other protected mangrove areas have been designated in India, Malaysia (Sarawak), Indonesia and Australia (Queensland).

Man-made wetlands

Thanks largely to the demise of 'natural' wetlands, accidentally produced and even artificial wetlands are increasingly prominent in developed countries. Indeed the distinction between the two is often confused, as in the case of the Norfolk Broads, which for the purposes of waterfowl counts are accepted as 'natural waters' [48].

Man-made wetlands include reservoirs, ponds and lagoons, extraction pits and waterways. Many — such as the extensive reservoirs around London — are close to dense concentrations of population, which increases their educational, scientific and recreational value; over 120 bird species have been recorded at Staines Reservoirs near London's Heathrow Airport. Similarly, the Unterer Inn Reservoirs in West Germany attract large populations of ducks and waders. Breeding species include night heron, purple heron and hobby.

Man-made wetlands have become some of the most important wildlife habitats in Western Europe. The Norfolk Broads are classified by Britain's Nature Conservancy Council as one of the nation's 'grade one' wildlife habitats. Many reservoirs support nationally important populations of wintering waterfowl, but these cannot fulfill many of the other important ecological functions of the natural wetlands which might have been destroyed in their construction.

"In actual fact the loss of wetlands has been so great that virtually any body of water is of some conservation importance", observes Dr Chris Tydeman of World Wildlife Fund-UK. Tydeman feels it important that planners and the public do not let the apparently rich birdlife of such artificial bodies of water distract their attention from the losses of more diverse habitats and species which occur when natural wetlands disappear. "The conservation of purely natural or semi-natural wetlands will no longer provide sufficient protection for wetland and aquatic species", maintains Tydeman, a view underlining the importance of artificial areas in the developed world. Indeed, Abberton Reservoir, in Essex (England), is actually listed as a site of international importance.

The recently increased popularity of garden and park ponds in Britain has been credited with the conservation of previously declining amphibian populations. A study in Sussex showed that about 15% of gardens had ponds [49]. Assuming that half were used as breeding sites, Tydeman suggests that the frog population is about seven animals per hectare, equivalent to the population of this group in the 1950s before the massive declines associated with habitat destruction reduced densities to perhaps 2% of this level. Today the survival of the common frog, the common toad, and the smooth and great crested newts relies to a great extent on artificial wetlands in Britain.

Even lagoons associated with sewage farms are important to wildlife, especially in winter when the lagoons are less likely to freeze over than natural bodies of water. The 'Rieselfelder', or sewage farm, in Münster, West Germany, and that at Jerez de la Frontera in Spain are both important for migratory and some breeding birds.

Flooded and abandoned sand, gravel, clay, coal and salt extraction pits are increasingly important wildlife habitats. Vegetation has established distinct zones of species in many cases, and sites are important both for plants and animals. Rarities such as the dune helleborine (*Epipactis dunensis*) grow in the salt extraction pits of Cheshire, England. About 90 species of bird — half of Britain's breeding species — regularly breed in gravel pits. The little ringed plover (*Charadrius dubius*) is one example of a bird which has established as a breeding species in Britain largely because of artificial gravel pit habitats.

As commerce has used them less and less, so canals have assumed new importance as wetlands. A part of the Shropshire Union Canal in Britain has been designated a 'grade one' site by the Nature Conservancy Council. Lack of traffic allows the development of a marginal wetland flora, which makes for diverse habitats and increased wildlife populations. However, the renewed interest in canals for recreational activities, especially boating, may set back this type of development. Trampling by people and wash from boats reduces the emergent vegetation, while garbage and nutrients in the water may cause oxygen shortages.

Man's ability to create artificial wetlands has led developers to argue that it should be acceptable to destroy a natural wetland if it was replaced with an identical system elsewhere or if the damaged wetland was later recreated. The phosphate industry in North Carolina, for example, has invested heavily in the development of artificial wetland creeks, complete with saltmarsh zones mimicking the natural sequence. The industry hopes that all this will convince the state government and Army Corps of Engineers to allow it to extract phosphate, in return for guarantees that it will restore the habitat and so 'mitigate' the impacts of mining.

But acceptance of this concept of 'mitigation' would put all pristine wetland areas at risk. Scientists are not yet sure whether the complex functions of natural wetlands can be mimicked, even with the most detailed reconstruction efforts. But they *are* sure that the natural system can do the job for less money.

Chapter 4

Types of wetland II:
Peatlands and floodplains

When plants die they begin to decompose. With the help of microbes, the plant tissue oxidises, eventually into carbon dioxide and water. Where low temperature, high acidity, low nutrient supply, waterlogging and oxygen deficiency retard decomposition, the plant matter does not oxidise, but instead accumulates and is transformed into peat.

Mires — the world's peatlands

Peat is usually called 'peat' — and not 'organic soil layers' — when it is deeper than 40 cm. In mires (synonymous with peatlands), the rate of production of plant litter exceeds the rate of breakdown. Peat normally accumulates at a rate of 0.2-1.6 millimetres per year, depending on local environment, vegetation, climate and human influences, until eventually an equilibrium is reached when decay of the entire peat mass balances the rate of addition of fresh organic material.

It is not uncommon for peat to be more than 10 metres deep in coastal states in both tropical and temperate regions. Indeed, such depths have been found recently on subantarctic islands such as the Falklands/Malvinas [50]. Once thought to be almost entirely restricted to the high latitudes of the northern hemisphere, peatlands are now thought to cover at least 500 million hectares, and occur in all continents. Thick deposits can form in association with marsh and swamp, particularly in tropical and sub-tropical lakes, floodplains and coastal regions. But peat also produces distinctive wetland landscapes of bog, moor, muskeg and fen.

'Bogs' have a high water table maintained directly by rain and snow, which also maintains waterlogging and reduces oxygen levels. The rainfall leaches out base materials, making them low in nutrients, and the slow fermentation of organic matter produces acids. Where the peat covers wide tracts of terrain independent of the details of relief the formation is called 'blanket bog'. These are typical of coastal and upland areas of western Europe, the Kamchatka peninsula in the Soviet Union, southern Chile, southwest New Zealand, subantarctic islands, and parts of the tundra (the treeless zone between the Arctic icecap and the

Edward Maltby

Peat has been used to cook food and heat homes for centuries. In subantarctic islands like the Falklands/Malvinas, where peat is a major fuel, peat layers more than 10 metres deep can occur.

northern timber line) and taiga (the vast coniferous forests of subarctic North America and Eurasia).

Bogs are characterised by acid-loving vegetation such as cotton grass, purple moor grass, rushes, sedges and mosses. Of particular importance are the bog mosses — the *Sphagnum* species — which can hold more than 10 times their dry weight of water.

Peat is a 'sink' for plant remains, nutrients and carbon. Active peat bogs fix carbon continually, although some bogs, such as many in northwest Europe and in the pocosins (see below) of North Carolina, are probably no longer accumulating peat or carbon, and in some cases may be losing carbon deposited long ago.

The conversion of peatlands to agriculture changes them from carbon 'sinks' to carbon sources, and releases carbon into the atmosphere. Drained and disturbed wetlands tend to lose more stored carbon (and other elements) than can be fixed in the same amount of time [51]. Not only does this add more gaseous carbon to the atmosphere, and other elements — including heavy metals like lead, zinc and caesium — to drainage waters, but it also reduces their storage within peat deposits. The Okeechobee area of Florida is losing nine million tonnes of carbon per year, and the San Joaquin delta, California, eight million tonnes.

Country	Area (ha)	Country	Area (ha)
WESTERN EUROPE		China	4,200,000
Austria	22,000	Fiji	4,000
Belgium	18,000	Indonesia	17,000,000
Denmark	120,000	India	32,000
Finland	10,400,000	Israel	5,000
France	90,000	Japan	250,000
FRG	1,110,000	Korea (DPR)	136,000
Great Britain	1,580,000	Malaysia	2,500,000
Greece	5,000	Papua New Guinea	—
Iceland	1,000,000	Philippines	6,000
Ireland	1,180,000	Sri Lanka	2,500
Italy	120,000	Thailand	68,000
Luxembourg	200	Vietnam	183,000
Netherlands	280,000		
Norway	3,000,000	**CENTRAL AMERICA**	
Spain	6,000	British Honduras	68,000
Sweden	7,000,000	Costa Rica	37,000
Switzerland	55,000	Cuba	767,000
		El Salvador	9,000
EASTERN EUROPE		Honduras	453,000
Bulgaria	1,000	Jamaica	21,000
Czechoslovakia	30,750	Nicaragua	371,000
GDR	489,000	Panama	787,000
Hungary	30,000	Puerto Rico	10,000
Poland	1,300,000	Trinidad and Tobago	1,000
Romania	7,000		
Soviet Union	150,000,000	**SOUTH AMERICA**	
Yugoslavia	100,000	Argentina	45,000
		Bolivia	900
AFRICA		Brazil	1,500,000
Angola	—	Chile	1,047,000
Burundi	14,000	Colombia	339,000
Congo	290,000	Falkland/Malvinas Is.	1,151,000
Guinea	525,000	French Guiana	162,000
Ivory Coast	32,000	Guyana	813,880
Lesotho	—	Surinam	113,000
Liberia	40,000	Uruguay	3,000
Madagascar	197,000	Venezuela	1,000,000
Malawi	91,000		
Mozambique	—	**NORTH AMERICA**	
Rwanda	80,000	Canada	150,000,000
Senegal	1,500	USA — Alaska	49,400,000
Uganda	1,420,000	USA — S of 49°N	10,240,000
Zaire	—		
Zambia	1,106,000	**THE PACIFIC**	
		Australia (Queensland)	15,000
ASIA		New Zealand	150,000
Bangladesh	60,000		

Areas of peatland by country. Source: Bord na Mona 1984.

Complete cultivation of the area of pocosins in North Carolina currently owned by corporate agriculture would release seven million tonnes annually [52]. This process poses questions of global concern. The planet is already threatened by increasing loads of atmospheric CO_2 given off by the burning of fossil fuels, forest clearance and intensified agriculture. In a 'greenhouse effect', the CO_2 could trap solar radiation, raise average world temperatures, cause the polar ice caps to melt, raise sea levels and hasten desertification [53].

The burning of fossil fuels releases about five billion tonnes of carbon per year. An estimated 30 million tonnes of carbon a year is being added to the atmosphere by peat fuel use and a further 10 million tonnes derives from oxidation of peat harvested for horticultural use (assuming an annual rate of oxidation of 25% of the amount harvested). Organic soils probably store 500 times the amount of carbon released from burning fossil fuels, and peatlands alone may store at least 500 billion tonnes of carbon (obtained by multiplying the estimate of Bellamy and Pritchard that was based on 150 million hectares by three and assuming an average carbon content in dry matter of 50%) [54]. Any discussion of what might happen to the planet's atmospheric carbon balance if wetlands suddenly ceased to exist is largely speculation, but it is clear that their buffering role in radiation balance and climatic control is of global importance. Agricultural conversion adds to the more direct danger of carbon released when peat is burned for energy or when horticultural peat is oxidised [55]. There is more and more evidence to show that drainage, recreation and other economic activities in and around peatlands are responsible for the growing numbers of accidental peat fires.

In some wet coastal regions and in uplands with high rainfall, deep mires have formed with an elevated centre and frequently a distinct "hollow-hummock" surface. These 'raised bogs' are found in Europe, the Soviet Union, Hokkaido, North America, in the tropical lowlands of Indonesia, Malaysia and Brazil, and in the temperate regions of Chile, Argentina, New Zealand and the subantarctic islands.

In Britain the vegetation of an actively growing raised bog is dominated by heather-clad or cotton grass hummocks and *Sphagnum*-carpeted hollows or open water pools. But other plants often vary the pattern — the carnivorous sundews (*Drosera* spp.), bog asphodel (*Narthecium ossifragum*), cranberry (*Oxycoccus palustris*), bog rosemary (*Andromeda polifolia*), white-beak sedge (*Rhynchospora alba*), and the rarer cloudberry (*Rubus chamaemorus*).

The depth of peat in raised bogs (generally 4-12 metres) has made them prime candidates for exploitation for energy or horticultural uses. Mechanised peat cutting has made massive inroads in recent years into some of the finest examples of raised bogs in Ireland. Elsewhere, excavation, drainage and recreational pressure have dramatically reduced or altered these wetlands. The high moisture content and low bearing strength of the peat makes raised bogs and deep blanket peat extremely vulnerable to trampling. Nowhere is the problem better illustrated than in the serious erosion problems associated with long distance footpaths in the North Yorkshire Moors and the Pennines of northern England.

More intensive grazing and burning of the moorland, along with increased levels of acid pollution and more accidental summer fires, have all accelerated the erosion of blanket and raised bogs in Britain and elsewhere in Europe. On the North Yorkshire Moors in the drought year of 1976, 11 sq km of moorland were destroyed by peat fires started by hikers.

Degradation of bogs may be due to a natural cycle of development and decay; it may be the result of a climate drier now than when the bogs began forming. But the syndrome has been amplified by increased peripheral drainage and intensified land use. Clearly, losses to human exploitation are not necessarily going to be replaced by natural processes of recovery.

Strange bog patterns have developed in regions of permafrost and frequent frost action. These include the remarkable geometry of frost wedge polygons, 'palsa bogs' (peat covered mounds or hills covered in cotton grass, sedges, mosses and sometimes shrubs) and string or 'aapa bogs', which form a mosaic of ridges and hollows, developed by the influence of ice movements and waterlogging. *Sphagnum*, cotton grass and sedges are the most common plants, but horsetails and bogbean (*Menyanthes*) are also found. In the taiga of the Northern hemisphere, larch, black spruce, pine, birch, alder and sallows may grow on the bog surface. Extreme waterlogging in the summer causes many tall trees to lean, producing spectacular 'drunken forests'.

The muskeg terrain of the northern peatlands is extremely difficult to cross in summer, but because of the strategic importance of these regions, a whole range of specialised military vehicles with low pressure traction have been devised.

As the climate becomes drier and bogs dry out at the surface in summer, an open woodland can develop on peat. Tree remains buried in European peatlands show that different types of forests have formed at different times. Some of the most intriguing forested bogs occur in the warm southern United States in a temperate climate not normally associated with bog formation. These southern bogs are called 'pocosins' and occur on broad flat divides between rivers and sounds along the southeast coastal plain, where they cover more than 1.2 million hectares. They were formed by the Holocene (beginning about 10,000 years ago) rise in sea level impeding drainage and increasing

A 'drunken forest' in the muskeg of Alaska. Bogs in the far north support larch, black spruce, pine, birch, alder and sallows; waterlogging in the summer causes tall trees to lean, producing these 'drunken forests'.

sedimentation [56]. The vegetation is dominated by evergreen shrubs of pond pine and bushes which produce a dense community difficult to penetrate. Nevertheless, the rare plants and high habitat value for a wide range of animals repays the effort of those who succeed. By 1980, less than a third of the original area of these bogs remained.

Fens. Mires which are fed by groundwater or interior drainage into hollows — rather than by precipitation — produce wetlands higher in nutrient content than bogs but still able to accumulate peat. The combination of more nutrients and lower acidity results in 'fens' supporting a very different vegetation, often with a luxuriant and species-rich cover of reeds, sedges and herbs. Often fed by chalky waters from groundwater, springs or hillside flushes, they are common throughout Europe, parts of North America, low latitude mountains and parts of Australia and New Zealand. Attractive broadleaved herbs often grow in association with these fens.

The value of peat. The use of peat as a fuel is well-known; it is and has been an important fuel for domestic heating and cooking for centuries (see Chapter 9). Peat-fuelled power stations in Ireland, the Soviet Union and Finland have increased peat's scope for energy production, and countries throughout the Third World are being encouraged to use their own peat both to reduce the loss of forests through cutting for fuelwood and to save on imported oil and coal [56a].

But peat has a wide range of additional values. Like other wetlands, peatlands absorb excess water. Peat provides a growth medium for specialised and rare plants such as sundew, Venus flytrap and other insect trappers. It filters and purifies water, and holds nutrients and heavy metals such as caesium and lead.

Bogs themselves are of great scientific interest and value. By providing an environment in which organic matter accumulates in discrete layers and decomposes extremely slowly, peat provides scientists with a record of the planet dating far back into prehistory. Pollen and much larger remains of plants, such as tree trunks which testify to previous forests, have allowed the reconstruction of the prehistoric landscape. Acid, waterlogged bogs have preserved vital archaeological and human remains.

For example, trackways built by prehistoric man have been found in the Somerset Levels in England. Remarkably preserved corpses have been found in Denmark and in Cheshire, England. The anatomy, intestinal remains, clothing and associated vegetation of the Cheshire bog man discovered in 1984 is helping piece together the way of life and environment of his prehistoric culture to a degree not previously possible. The apparent cause of death — ritual garrotting — added not only intrigue but the possibility that future finds might add significantly to our knowledge of the evolution of human society. As methods of scientific analysis improve — such as the radiocarbon dating of progressively smaller samples of peat and the magnetic 'fingerprinting' of materials — it is imperative that the peat from which the evidence will be taken by future generations is preserved intact.

Peat also has its agricultural and gardening uses. Horticultural peat, used as a growing medium, is much sought after, and its extraction provides jobs in Ireland, the Somerset Levels of southwestern England, Sweden, Finland, the states of Minnesota and Florida in the United States, and the Soviet Union. Many peatlands have been and are being cultivated directly, but this invariably destroys the resource. In Florida, peat deposits are disappearing particularly rapidly to satisfy the gardening fashions of the fast-growing coastal towns.

Peat provides the raw materials for various chemical products such as alcohol, humic acids, waxes, resins, oils and tar, binders and cellulose. According to Michael Blackwood of the Petroleum Corporation of Jamaica, one tonne of sawgrass peat can yield 23 kg of tar, 18 kg of ammonia (NH_3), 11 litres of light oil, 360 kg of coke, 150 litres of water, and 40 cubic metres of gas.

Despite all this activity, the full chemical potential of peat has yet to be realised, and investigations continue. It would be a tragedy if science found important new uses for peat, only to find that in many places there was too little peat left to take advantage of these discoveries [57]. Peat is used as an absorbent material in sewage management and in air pollution monitoring and control. As it is lightweight, fibrous and conducts electricity poorly, it has found uses in thermal insulation and construction materials. *Sphagnum* peat from Ginini Bog in New South Wales, Australia, was used as packing in munitions.

The antiseptic qualities of peat acids and other biologically active substances have long been recognised in Europe. Peat bathing helped to establish St Moritz in the Swiss Alps as a spa. At 13 Czechoslovakian spas, including the largest at Trebon, peat treatments (peloids) are used as part of the therapy in rheumatology, urology, neurology, gynaecology, gastroenterology and in other metabolic diseases. Peloid application is in the form of packs, mud baths and gynaecological tampons. In Britain, researchers are investigating the potential for using *Sphagnum* moss in medicine, primarily in dressings.

Floodplains

The periodic flooding of land between river channels and valley sides is a common feature of the lower reaches of rivers throughout the world, and produces a complex variety of riverside wetlands, depending on the climate, the water regime and the form of the floodplain. The fertile floodplains of the Nile, the Tigris-Euphrates, the Indus and the Huang Ho were the foundation of great civilisations.

The natural lay of the land helps to control the depth, timing and duration of flooding. Permanent or semi-permanent areas of standing water may be left after the recession of floodwaters in the form of oxbows and other depressions. These waters are often very shallow, but can be important dry season refuges for fish, which frequently spawn on the temporarily flooded land. They are important wildlife habitat and a key resource for many subsistence farming communities in Africa, Asia and South America. Specialised local terms reflect the special significance of floodplain areas in the lives of many people.

In the United States, periodically flooded areas produced the bottomland hardwood forests which once covered vast areas of the floodplains of the southeastern, eastern and central United States. The largest contiguous areas occur in the lower Mississippi River Valley; this wetland type still covers more than 23.5 million hectares in the United States. Species composition varies according to the flooding regime. In the southeast, the wettest areas are dominated by bald cypress and water tupelo. Black willow, silver maple and occasionally cottonwood are prominent in semi-permanently inundated or saturated zones, with

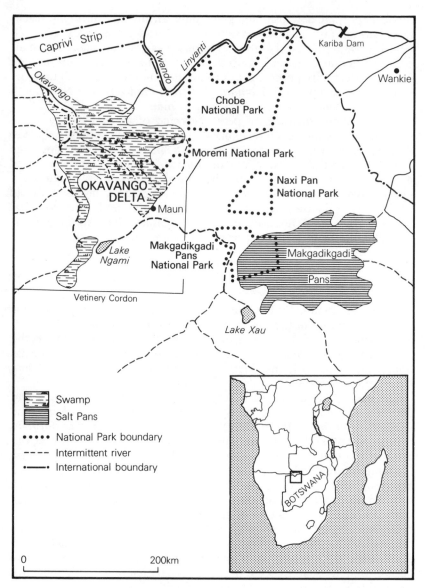

The Okavango swamp of Botswana.

oaks, ash, elm and hickories more characteristic of the seasonally flooded margins.

However, the riverside marshes and forests which once characterised the 'fringing floodplains' of rivers in Europe and North America have now largely disappeared through the deepening of river channels, the building of levees and the development of riverside land.

One such forest is the Hainburg near Vienna, one of the largest areas of riverine forest left in Europe, and listed under the Convention on Wetlands of International Importance (or Ramsar convention — see Chapter 7) as of international importance. It is regularly flooded by snowmelt waters and supports an extremely rich wildlife, including three-quarters of the tree species found in Europe, over 200 species of breeding and migratory birds (including sea eagles, storks and spoonbills), over 40 species of fish, and other species such as tree frogs, tortoises and otters. Yet even this last vestige of a formerly much more extensive wetland forest would have been lost had not the Supreme Court of Austria ruled in January 1985 against the construction of a hydroelectric dam near the Czechoslovakian border.

The world's remaining major seasonal floodplains are now limited to the tropics and subtropics. But in Africa, woodfuel gathering, overgrazing, drought, and efforts to control river flow are rapidly degrading these ecologically and environmentally important systems, for example along the Senegal, Niger and Benue rivers. Fringing floodplain forests continue to disappear too in South America and Asia.

Some floodplains support many lakes. The Grand Lac of the Lower Mekong in the Khmer Republic changes in area from 2,500 sq km in the dry season to 11,000 sq km in flood [58]. Eighteen major lakes are formed in the Inner Niger Delta during the dry period; the internal delta of the Magdalena in Colombia supports 800 lakes. Because sediment can fill them relatively quickly, floodplain lakes tend to be ephemeral. Spreading wetland vegetation can speed this process, as on the Danube, where lakes have been turned into reed-dominated ponds.

'Inland deltas'. 'Deltas' are usually defined as areas where rivers spread and divide before entering the sea. But geological features can cause rivers to spill across wide inland plains and divide into multiple channels, forming so-called 'inland deltas'.

The vast Okavango delta of northwest Botswana has formed where the Okavango River meets a deep layer of Kalahari sand. The river's velocity is reduced, and its crystal clear waters form the maze of channels, islands and lagoons described as "one of Africa's most beautiful remaining wildernesses" [59]. Floating and submerged plants enrich the open waters, papyrus and reeds dominate the 'swamps' or marsh, and grassland dominates the seasonally inundated floodplain between the saturated zone and the dry uplands.

Country	Levee	Floodplain	Depression lagoon or swamps	Channels and side arms
Benin	Tikpa	Ti		
Brazil		Varzea	Lago de varzea	Parana
Kampuchea		Veal	Beng	Prek
Colombia			Cienaga	Cano
India			Bheel	Jheel
Rumania			Ghiol: japse	
Senegal	Fonde	Oualo	Vindo	Tiangol
Sri Lanka			Villus	
Sudan		Toiche		

Glossary of terms for floodplain features. Source: R.L. Welcomme 1979.

These are important wildlife habitats, supporting crocodile and fish, Pel's Fishing Owl (which can catch fish weighing 2 kg), egrets (including the rare Slaty egret), herbivores like the red lechwe (whose movements are closely linked with the seasonally available floodplain grassland), and other animals which depend on the water for their survival, such as elephant and buffalo.

About 70% of the 40,000 people who live in and around the delta depend entirely on the land and the resources it provides — the Yei for fishing and the Tswana for herding. Many wild plants are harvested for food, shelter and other uses, including alcoholic drinks. Crop cultivation has become more important in recent years and increasingly threatens the remaining marshlands where burning and clearance makes available land generally more productive than the drier margins.

Other important inland deltas include those of the Niger River, the Kafue Flats of Zambia, and the Magdalena River in Colombia, whose deltaic confluence with the San Jorge and Cauca rivers covers over 20,000 sq km. The Paraguay River below the Gran Pantanal floodplain and the Paraná River after its confluence with the Paraguay also form inland deltas. The delta at the confluence of the Amazon and Tapajós covers 50,000 sq km [60]. In all these cases, the environment on which local people depend for their resources is threatened by 'development' schemes.

In some areas the terrain is so flat that seasonal rainfall can produce flooding over large areas. Such 'sheet flooding' can be supplemented by water spilling over river banks, but this may occur weeks or even months later. The erosion of complex, connecting channels can give the entire area the appearance of a delta.

There are extensive sheet flooding regions in the basin of the Chari-Logone River basin in southern Chad. They sustain large populations of wild ungulates (hooved mammals) and other animals; as the waters recede, local people grow sorghum and rice, and graze their domestic livestock. Floodplain grasses can produce up to 10 tonnes of dry matter per hectare and carry 1-2 head of cattle per hectare in the non-flood period. Some of the largest sheet-flood regions occur in South America: the Gran Pantanal of the Paraguay River, where shallow interconnecting lakes and wetland complexes can cover up to 100,000 sq km in some years, and the Apure-Arauca tributaries of the Orinoco in Venezuela, which produce a floodplain of 70,000 sq km.

Coastal delta floodplains. When a river reaches the flat floodplains of the coast, its flow is checked and the sediment it carries settles. The river spreads out through the land it is itself creating, forming a many-mouthed delta. A prime example is the Ganges-Brahmaputra delta, which continues to develop in its Bangladesh section, where more than 90,000 sq km of land is liable to flooding, in addition to 14,000 sq km of permanent open inland waters [61].

Other examples include the Huang Ho (Yellow River) in China, the Senegal River, the 31,000 sq km delta of the Irrawaddy River of Burma, and the increasingly modified regime of the Mekong, where nearly 30% of the total area of 74,000 sq km is no longer flooded, largely because of artificial channel constructions. The Nile and the Mississippi deltas are both actively eroding away over large areas — in the first case due to reductions in river silt since the construction of the Aswan Dam, and in the second to increased flood control measures within the delta, dense canal construction, land subsidence and a natural tendency for flows to shift westwards towards the Atchafalaya channel.

Coastal wetlands are ecologically and environmentally diverse because of the gradual, often fluctuating and dynamic boundaries between salt, brackish and freshwaters. Salt water may penetrate considerable distances upstream, but boundary patterns vary with water regimes and geological forms. These patterns influence not only vegetation, but also animal behaviour, such as the degree to which marine species can range into the food-rich wetlands.

Floodplain wetland forests. Forested wetlands on floodplains inundated only by seasonal flooding differ from 'swamps', but in reality the two often merge over a wide transition zone. Both are frequently part of a complex mosaic determined by local variations in topography and drainage. They lie at the interface between the river and the adjacent uplands, which sheds runoff and materials. These forests are also part of the chain of ecological and physical transfers between upstream and downstream areas. Like many other wetland ecosystems, their vegetation, soils and wildlife fall into zones according to variations in flooding regime.

The floodplain forest is a key element in natural flood protection and water quality maintenance. It is one of the richest of wildlife habitats and at times of flood provides spawning and nursery grounds for a variety of fish, including carp, catfish and bass. Yet between 1959 and 1964, 400,000 hectares were cleared in the Mississippi delta region; 45,000 hectares per year were converted almost exclusively to soybean cultivation in northern Louisiana alone. Present forested wetland loss in the state is still about 1% annually, although federal and state agencies are steadily responding to the demands of conservation groups (through the courts) to restrain landowners still intent on their destruction.

We do not know how much riverside wetland remains in the Third World, or its rate of loss, but there is little doubt that it is fast disappearing — for woodfuel in Senegal, Mali, Nigeria and elsewhere in drought-stricken Africa, and more generally as the pace of aid-inspired development accelerates along economic lines which include little analysis of ecological and environmental losses.

Other wetlands

Once the generally accepted catagories are exhausted, defining 'wetlands' becomes a tediously legalistic business, depending on the usage of the local lawmakers, authorities or conservation groups. The US Fish and Wildlife Service does not define permanently flooded deepwater areas as wetland. These zones, generally deeper than 1.8 metres, are defined as 'deepwater habitats' "since water and not air is the principal medium in which dominant organisms must live" [62].

But shallow lakes and ponds are considered wetlands by many authorities, and coastal waters to a depth of six metres are included by some. Thus reefs and aquatic beds of plants such as eelgrass (*Zostera*) and *Thalassia* seagrass would fall into this wide definition. There are also wetlands which may have no higher vegetation at all: rocky shores and bottoms; shores of mud, silt or sand; flats; and stream and river beds.

Chapter 5

Wetlands and water quality

More people using more water for more purposes have made it ever more difficult to provide enough water for drinking, irrigation and industry.

Clean water is often expensive enough in industrialised nations; in developing countries the costs can be prohibitive, and dirty water brings disease and early death. Diarrhoea, often caused by bad water, kills 25 million people each year in the Third World, and 80% of the world's disease is linked to unsafe water and poor sanitation [63]. Wetlands, once regarded as sources of disease, can actually help maintain water quality, promote the rapid growth of plants, absorb toxic metals and chemicals, clean up polluted water, and even act as natural sewage treatment plants. One wetland scientist who has spent much time in African wetlands, John Gaudet, has likened a papyrus swamp to a septic tank depositing nutrients in the detritus below the floating vegetation mat.

Controlling the flow of nutrients

Excessive amounts of nutrients such as nitrogen and phosphorus can cause rapid plant and algal growth — a process known as 'eutrophication'. As the plants die, their decomposition consumes oxygen from the water and fish can die from lack of oxygen. This is a particular danger in water near agricultural land which receives large doses of nitrogen and phosphorus in fertiliser runoff.

Wetland plants can absorb these nutrients. This would not in itself ensure their eventual removal from the water, because the plants might re-release it as they decomposed or recycled biological material. But wet, low-oxygen wetland soils favour 'denitrification' by certain bacteria, i.e. transforming nitrates or nitrites into molecular nitrogen or a gaseous oxide which diffuses into the atmosphere. This mechanism can remove between 40% and 98% of nitrogen from wetlands.

Phosphorus and other nutrients are removed in different ways. Plants taking up phosphorus store it only temporarily, releasing it when they decompose. No microorganisms can transform phosphorus into a gas. Nevertheless, large amounts of phosphorus are inactivated by chemical bonding to inorganic ions, mainly aluminium and iron. Wetlands with mainly mineral soils and high amorphous aluminium content — such as swamps — are better phosphorus sinks than peatlands, but generally do not retain as much phosphate as terrestrial ecosystems. When saturated with phosphorus they export rather than retain the nutrient [64].

Removing toxins

Wetland plants can remove heavy metals, pesticides and other toxins from water, fixing them at least temporarily in their own tissues. In theory, this could harm creatures higher up the food chain. For example, plants in a marsh can take up mercury, periwinkles feeding on the plants can concentrate high levels of mercury, and fish and birds even higher levels. But wetlands have various biological, chemical, biochemical and physical processes (still imperfectly understood) which can immobilise, transform and fix contaminants, preventing high proportions of them from flowing out or entering groundwater or the food chain. The efficiency of heavy metal removal varies from 20-100%.

Waste water treatment

James Gosselink and his colleagues at the Center for Wetland Resources at Louisiana State University suggest that the 'natural' waste treatment functions of southeastern US tidal marshes are worth $123,500 per hectare, calculated on the cost of replacing these functions with artificial treatment facilities. In some southeastern states, wetlands are actually being used as 'tertiary' waste water treatment facilities. In other words, water entering the wetlands has already undergone two treatments to remove most contaminants, but is still contaminated by a number of microorganisms and chemicals.

Wetlands can transform, fix and render harmless viruses, coliform bacteria (from faeces) and suspended solids normally left after secondary sewage treatment. They can do this with minimal dependence on mechanical equipment, other than a few simple pumps, so the system has a low failure rate.

Among the natural wetlands that have been considered as natural 'sewerage systems': cypress domes (roughly circular cypress swamps occupying shallow, saucer-shaped depressions); cypress strands (more extensive and diffuse freshwater streams flowing through a shallow forested depression on a gently sloping plain); brackish marshes; freshwater tidal marshes; freshwater inland marshes and bogs; and man-made wetlands.

The concept of using Florida cypress swamps as natural tertiary

These figures underline how efficient this technique could be in areas of relatively low population density.

Measure of water quality	Pond with hyacinths		Pond without hyacinths	
	Inflow	Outflow	Inflow	Outflow
Biochemical oxygen demand	22.0	7.0	27.0	30.0
Suspended solids	43.0	6.0	42.0	46.0
Total nitrogen	4.4	1.1	4.5	4.5
Total phosphorus	5.0	3.8	4.8	4.6

Treatment capability of water hyacinths fed partly treated wastewater (in mg/litre). Source: modified from Wolverton and McDonald 1975).

Measure of water quality	Water flowing into wetland	Water flowing out of wetland
Biochemical oxygen demand	520	16
Suspended solids	860	57
Nitrogen	36	4
Faecal coliform bacteria count per 100 millilitres	3,000	21

Treatment performance of an artificial wetland system on Long Island, New York (in mg/litre). Source: modified from data of Small 1972, report by Fritz and Helle 1978).

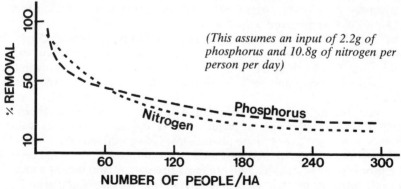

(This assumes an input of 2.2g of phosphorus and 10.8g of nitrogen per person per day)

Estimated removal efficiency for nitrogen and phosphorus by one hectare of wetland. Source: modified from Nichols 1983.

Edward Maltby

The remarkable wetland water hyacinth (above) is an effective pollution filter. Considered a nuisance in many countries because it spreads rapidly over open water (right), it can filter out toxic metals and pesticides, often in a matter of hours. It can also be used for compost, animal feed, conversion to biogas or to make paper and board.

treatment centres for domestic waste waters was developed in 1973 by Howard Odum and Katherine Ewel at the Center for Wetlands, University of Florida. About 98% of all nitrogen and 97% of all phosphorus was removed before waste waters entered the groundwater, which itself remained well within Federal Drinking Water Quality Standards. Cost-effectiveness varies with exact site conditions, but studies in Waldo, Florida, found that tertiary treatment by cypress wetlands would cost only 40% as much as a physical/chemical treatment plant.

Odum and his colleagues believe this use of wetlands gives them a greater long term economic value than if the same wetlands were drained and given over to pine plantations. Using wetlands this way not only gets the sewage treated, but the increased flows of water increases the productivity of the wetlands, reduces fire danger and means a more reliable recharge of underground aquifers. The trees at Waldo grew 2.6 times faster in the treatment area compared with trees in wetlands not being used in this way, a finding which raises the possibility of coupling

Edward Maltby

'treatment wetlands' to logging operations.

It has been estimated that forests suitable for sewage treatment exist for 35% of the waste water treatment facilities in Florida [65]. While supportive of the research, however, the federal and state regulatory agencies still have not allowed widespread implementation of the approach. More research is needed to explore possible ecological and environmental knock-on effects in the wetlands themselves, and possible dangers associated with the accumulation of potentially hazardous materials in the natural ecosystem.

Using wetland plants. Aquatic plants are proving an asset in the treatment of sewage and polluted water. In the Florida cypress trials, duckweed (*Lemna* spp.) removed almost half the nitrogen, 67% of the phosphorus and nearly all the heavy metals. Duckweed grows rapidly (annual production levels in the subtropics exceed 4 kg/sq metre. There are real possibilities of using duckweed species as a biofertiliser, in biogas production (in which dung and vegetation are used to produce methane for cooking and heating) and for synthesising protein from wastewater. Groups in both the United States and West Germany have done experimental work on making protein from wastewater.

Water hyacinth (*Eichornia crassipes*) may prove useful in treating raw sewage. The plant is considered a nuisance in many parts of the world because it spreads rapidly over open water, restricts navigation, and reduces levels of oxygen in the water. A native of South America (called the 'Florida devil' in that continent and the 'Bengal terror' in India), it has spread to 80 countries in the last century.

But it is now extensively used as a pollution filter. The plant absorbs nutrients such as nitrogen, phosphorus, potassium and other substances directly from water. It can take out more than 75% of the lead in contaminated water in just 24 hours, and also absorbs cadmium, nickel, chromium, zinc, copper and iron, and pesticides and other toxic wastes. Work in Mississippi in the 1970s showed that water hyacinth could remove 92% of nitrogen, 60% of phosphorus and 97% of biochemical oxygen demand in seven days of exposure to the pollutants. It has been found particularly valuable in the treatment of the ponds in which sewage is allowed to oxidise.

Removing the water hyacinth from the water removes the pollutants permanently from the aquatic system. Ray Dinges, a biologist with the Texas Department of Health, estimates that a hyacinth pond needs about five days to clean up the same quantity of wastewater that a conventional sewage treatment facility could manage in six hours. But because of the high energy costs involved in operating conventional treatment plants, the hyacinth ponds may treat the same volume of waste for less than half the cost.

The city of San Diego, California, is spending $3.5 million cultivating water hyacinth for wastewater treatment. Within a decade the city could be processing 190 million litres of sewage a day using water hyacinth [66]. At Disney World in Orlando, Florida, water hyacinth is used to clean effluent and provide water which can then be recycled to the park. The cattail-dominated Brillion Marsh in Wisconsin has received domestic sewage since 1923, and removes 80% of biochemical oxygen demand, 86% of coliform bacteria, 51% of nitrates, 40% of carbonates, 44% of the turbidity (cloudiness), 29% of suspended solids, and 13% of the total phosphorus.

Third World applications. The greatest potential for the use of aquatic plants and wetlands in wastewater treatment is in the Third World, where the cost of energy and the cost of building and running conventional treatment plants often prevents such plants being built. Those that are built often break down and are never repaired.

The Central Leather Research Institute of India has used water hyacinth experimentally to clean tannery effluents which are damaging groundwater resources in Madras. In Malaysia, the aquatic plant *Azolla* is being used to treat wastewater both from sugar refineries and from a rubber processing plant. *Azolla* is used as an important bio-fertiliser in the Pearl River delta region of China.

Calcutta's sewage has undergone natural purification in the complex of wetlands east of the city for at least 50 years. The 4,000 hectares of lakes and pools of the 'Salt Lakes' marshland have proved highly efficient oxidation ponds, and water treatment is augmented by water hyacinth. The ponds are also stocked with fish, mostly carp and tilapia, providing employment for 20,000 fishermen and producing an annual catch of 6,000 tonnes. Coliform bacteria from faeces are reduced by 99.9% in the well-stocked ponds. The West Bengal Department of Fisheries is now doing research to try and work out why and how the wetland can be such an effective cleaner of waste water and producer of fish [67]. Such knowledge could then be used to extend the system to other locations in India and other parts of the world, especially those where protein is in short supply.

Water hyacinth has other fringe benefits. The plant is rich in — and can efficiently extract from water — the sort of plant nutrients which, in excessive amounts, can deplete oxygen in water. The ash of the plant, which contains 30% potash, 7% phosphoric acid and 13% lime, makes an excellent fertiliser. Its value has been proven in Sudan, where it has increased peanut production by over 30%.

The Jorhat Institute in Jorhat, India, suggests that India could obtain five million tonnes of compost from water hyacinth with an equivalent value of more than 10,000 tonnes of nitrogen, 55,000 tonnes of phosphorus and 125 tonnes of potash, worth more than $1 million. Other possible uses for the plant include conversion to biogas (up to 40 litres of gas can be produced from 90 kg fresh weight of plant), animal feed (the plant is 17% protein and 26% carbohydrate) and various paper and board products. Dr Gopalakrishna Thyagarajam, Director of the Institute, argues that the water hyacinth's properties as a converter of solar energy into biomass makes it a basic resource for rural industry [68].

Removal of suspended sediments

By slowing the velocity of water flow, and increasing the 'residence time' of water in the ecosystem, wetlands enable biological, physical and chemical changes to occur in the water.

Large sediment loads can quickly silt up rivers and reservoirs, dramatically shortening the lives of hydroelectric projects. High turbidity in estuaries can reduce the production of phytoplankton by reducing the sunlight reaching these organisms. If the suspended sediment has a high organic carbon content, then its decomposition consumes oxygen, cutting the supply for fish and other organisms. Nutrients, heavy metals and pesticides can be adsorbed by the sediment particles and transported by them in the water.

Slowed velocity not only cleans the water but helps build up the land surface in subsiding coastlines, such as the Mississippi and Ganges deltas. In estuaries, the action of saltwater mixing with freshwater causes the sediment to form into aggregates (clumps) and settle. Where land is subsiding, as in the Mississippi delta, sediment deposition is essential to maintain the coastal marshlands. Sediment generally builds up at 2-4 mm per year in areas with established vegetation, but on bare mudflats and areas of spreading cordgrass (*Spartina*) buildup can be as much as 37-45.5 mm per year. Considerable amounts of nitrogen and phosphorus may be removed from the water with the sediment deposited in streamside marshes.

The ability of marsh vegetation to make water clearer and to filter contaminants from dredged material is important to the US Army Corps of Engineers, which has to deal with the practical problems posed by the runoff from disposed dredge material. At sites near Georgetown, South Carolina and Pennville, New Jersey, slurry was passed through wetland vegetation such as reeds (*Phragmites australis*), giant reedgrass (*Arundo donax*) and willows (*Salix* spp). The slurry was so well filtered that the resulting effluent was no more turbid than the rivers into which it was discharged.

Wetlands, water supply and aquifers

It is often claimed that wetlands can play important roles in recharging aquifers (layers of rock or soil which hold water), but there is little scientific evidence to support any general rules, because wetland types vary so enormously. Studies in Massachusetts found that most local wetlands were helping recharge aquifers, but elsewhere wetlands may in fact be sinks for water discharged from aquifers.

In either case, wetlands provide a hydrological buffer and regulate water flows; the benefits to humans are great. In Massachusetts, over 40% of wetlands are potential sources of drinking water, and many public wells are in the wetlands or very nearby [69]. Coastal wetlands maintain the water pressure in groundwater supplies, which is vital for keeping salt water from seeping into groundwater and contaminating it. The coastal morasses of Jamaica are a good example. So are the Florida wetlands, but there human interference with flow patterns, and overuse of the water, threatens to allow sea water into groundwater supplies.

Artificial systems

Ironically, as many nations are destroying their natural wetlands in the name of 'development', developed nation scientists, realising the value of these ecosystems, are working on ways to build artificial wetlands to mimic the functions of the real things. Artificial wetland systems are operating in the Netherlands, Hungary, Poland and Yugoslavia.

Kaethe Seidel of the Max Plank Institute in West Germany has developed an artificial marsh system consisting of bulrush (*Schoenoplectus lacustrus*) and reeds (*Phragmites australis*). Joost de Jong from the Netherlands has revealed a considerable reduction in phosphorus, nitrogen, biochemical oxygen demand and bacteria in the effluent of a marsh-reed wetland based on bulrush. The level of purification achieved in artificial wetlands is well illustrated in results obtained by Maxwell Small of the Brookhaven National Laboratory on Long Island. Recent work from that laboratory has shown that a marsh/pond system of eight hectares will clean 4.54 million litres of raw agricultural sewage per day.

Physical protection

About a quarter of the 100,000 cubic km of rainwater falling annually on the earth runs off as flood flow [70]. The cost of damage from floods in the United States alone averages $3-4 billion each year. But in countries like Bangladesh and India, floods regularly bring death and misery to overused and overpopulated floodplains — a warning to those intent on the intensified development of the African floodplains.

Wetlands can mitigate flooding in several ways. They store potential floodwaters, at least temporarily. They reduce floodwater peaks, and their very existence can assure that floodwaters from tributaries do not all reach the main river at the same time.

The value of these functions in protecting lives, property and crops is increasingly important around cities, where development means that more and more of the land surface — roads, packed earth, etc — is impervious to water. This increases the volume of runoff and the flood hazard. Yet humans are continually drawn to rivers by the flat fertile land, nearby water and easier transport and communication. Such settlement has both been made possible by and required the drainage of wetlands and the construction of levees and other devices to artificially control floods.

In the 48 contiguous states of the United States, more than 520,000 sq km — an area almost as large as France — has severe flooding problems. Most of this area is agricultural land which is either wetland or previously drained wetland. All wetlands in valleys or other depressions will store runoff. The Prairie Potholes in the Devils Lake Basin of North Dakota store nearly 75% of total runoff [71]. The peat bogs of northwest Europe and the northern United States act as sponges, soaking up the often heavy rainfall and slowly releasing water as a sustained base flow to streams. This not only reduces flood dangers, but helps provide a steady, reliable supply of water to farms and cities downstream.

The financial benefits of using natural wetlands for flood control was emphasised by the US Army Corps of Engineers in its work along the Charles River near Boston, Massachusetts. Proposals to alleviate flooding there included the building of reservoirs and extensive walls and dykes. Another possibility was simply to protect the 3,440 hectares of wetlands as natural water storage areas.

It was estimated that flood damage would increase by a minimum of $3 million per year if 40% of the Charles River wetlands were destroyed; if all the wetlands were removed, the figure would rise to $17 million annually [72]. This study put the value of the retained natural wetland at $1,203,000 a year — the difference between annual flood losses based on present land use and conditions, and projected flood losses by 1990 if 30% of valley storage ability of the wetlands was lost [73].

Saving the wetlands made financial sense, so in 1983 the Corps finished acquiring and setting up a protection regime for the Charles River basin wetlands. The project offers remarkable new insight into the roles of natural ecosystems. It came too late to prevent many environmentally disastrous flood control structures in the United States, but could provide a model for future policy, both there and in the Third World.

Storm protection. In a hurricane (or cyclone or typhoon: the same phenomenon by different names) it is not the wind that kills so much as the ocean surges and floods which usually accompany these storms. Hurricanes can produce storm surges up to 7.5 metres high, sending floods several kilometres inland. About 90% of hurricane deaths in the United States are caused by drowning. Some six million people are exposed to storm surge damage along the US Gulf and Atlantic coasts, and millions more in Australia, Bangladesh, China, India, Japan and Mexico are similarly prone.

While property damage from hurricanes is highest in the developed Northern nations prone to such storms, deaths and injury are usually highest in the poor tropical and sub-tropical nations, where larger numbers of people are exposed to the storms. Agriculture is also vulnerable to hurricane damage; the immediate destruction of crops can be followed by years of reduced yields caused by the salt deposited in plantations by storm surges. The vulnerability of many coastal

Tom Learmonth/Earthscan

Floods near Dacca, Bangladesh. One in seven Bangladeshis lives less than three metres above sea level. Their vulnerability to flooding from storm surges is worsened by the removal of coastal wetlands, which are natural buffers against storm waves.

communities is heightened by the removal of coastal wetlands for crops and habitation. These wetlands are natural buffers against storm surges. In industrialised countries, their protective function has been at least partly replaced by artificial sea barriers, and people have the benefit of early warning, training for evacuation and transport with which to evacuate.

But in the delta area of Bangladesh, vast numbers of people are exposed on lowlands long stripped of wetland vegetation. Some 15% of the nation's 100 million inhabitants live less than three metres above sea level. Eleven storms during the 1960s killed 54,000 people. The 1970 storm surge killed 150,000-300,000 people [74], and in June 1985 over 40,000 were drowned. (A study of the 1970 disaster found that about a third of the survivors saved themselves by clinging to trees — most of which have since been cut down.) As sediment brought down in the Ganges and Brahmaputra rivers forms new islands, people rush to live on them to take advantage of the rich soil for farming. Mangroves and other vegetation are never given a chance to grow.

The mangrove forest of the uncleared Sundarbans forest of Bangladesh and India acts as a coastal buffer, dampening the effects of

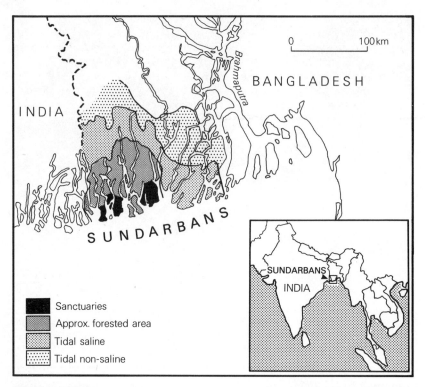

The Sundarbans.

storm waves which may exceed four metres in height. In recognition of their protective functions, the Bangladesh government is having mangroves planted or replanted in some areas to protect embankments and new land. Some 25,000 hectares have been planted to date, with another 40,000 scheduled before the end of the decade [75]. So important is the role of mangrove swamps in coastal protection in the Philippines that a Presidential Decree is meant to ensure the preservation of a 40 metre wide belt of mangroves along rivers and lakes, and a 100 metre wide belt facing bays and the sea.

But in much of the Third World, large tracts of mangrove are steadily being lost, much of it caused by very poor people desperate for farmland, woodfuel, charcoal to use or sell, or building poles and wood from which to make items for sale. Clearance controls must be sensitive to the needs of these users, who rarely have other sources of income.

In the United States, Federal Insurance Administration regulations state that insured communities shall prohibit the destruction of mangroves, or lose federal flood insurance. This has come too late for large areas of mangrove fringe cleared in Florida for resorts and other development. Mangrove clearance is proceeding apace in Australia, despite the growing awareness of their importance.

Fortunately, mangroves, saltmarshes and other wetland systems are capable of some self-repair. Because artificial sea defences and river levees are expensive to build and repair (in Britain, coastal defence constructions cost well over £1 million per km), no-cost natural alternatives begin to look very appealing. There is growing awareness that trees adapted to waterlogged conditions are effective in controlling bank erosion and that conserving or even replanting wetland vegetation may be the most cost-effective solution to erosion problems in both freshwater and marine environments.

Chapter 6

Wetlands and wildlife

Wetlands host a rich and diverse collection of plants and animals. They are a vast genetic resource, only a fraction of which has been studied, and a still smaller fraction tapped for human use. Wetlands have already yielded economically important species like rice, sago, oil palm, mangroves, crayfish, shrimp, oysters, caimans, waterfowl, fish and fur-bearing animals. They may yield even more important genetic material, as yet undiscovered.

The ways in which plants and animals have adapted to and depend on wetlands also makes them particularly vulnerable to man-made changes in wetlands. Many already rare and endangered species either live in wetlands or depend on them for survival. Some plants and animals exist only in a particular type of wetland; others spend just part of their life-cycle there, or visit for specific purposes such as resting, spawning or feeding. Other species — mostly waterfowl — move from one wetland to another in a set migratory pattern. Such migrations pose a particular challenge to resource managers because key habitats may be far apart, even separated by national boundaries.

Diversity — the key to wetland wealth

Wetlands offer different niches for wildlife, not only from one place to another but from one time to another. Parts of wetlands may be flooded at one time of year and dry at another, so fish and mammals use the same area at different times.

The rich productivity of wetlands allows them to sustain large populations of organisms dependent on one another. The endangered Everglades kite (*Rostrhamus sociabilas*), which is totally dependent on the apple snail (*Pomacea paludosa*), can survive in viable numbers in the isolated habitat of the Florida Everglades because the marsh can also support a large population of the snails.

Regional varieties and subspecies of plants, insects and other invertebrates are often confined to single wetlands in a given region. If the habitat is destroyed, the organism is destroyed. In Britain, the rare Ray's knotgrass (*Polygonum oxyspernum raii*) and sea purslane

(*Halimione portulacoides*) still grow in the Bridgewater Bay wetlands of southwest England, but *Halimione pedunculata* has not been seen in the saltmarshes of southern England for 50 years [76]. The swallowtail butterfly (*Papilio machaon brittanica*) is confined to the Bure Marshes and adjacent broadlands of eastern England.

Wetlands are rich in species endemic (restricted) to small geographical areas. The study of such species aids the study of evolution, allowing researchers to see how species evolve when isolated from other similar species. The Great Lakes (Victoria, Tanganyika, Nyasa/Malawi) of Africa are particularly rich in endemic fish, especially in cichlids, e.g. Mbuna and Utaka. In Lake Tanganyika, 214 species have been identified, of which 80% are endemic, but there are more in the other lakes (more than 700 altogether). Many of these species have evolved from a few 'parent' species, filling most of the ecological niches the lake has to offer.

About 9% of the 92 species of flowering plants found in Jamaica's Black River Lower Morass are endemic to Jamaica, 7% to the Greater Antilles and 3% to the West Indies. The morass hosts two genera, seven species and two subspecies of endemic birds. Endemism is a feature of a wide variety of wetland animals, such as the turtle *Erymnochelys madagascariensis* in Madagascar, the Kafue lechwe (*Kobus leche kafuensis*) in the Kafue Flats in Zambia and the black lechwe (*Kobus leche smithemani*) in the Benguelu basin of Zambia.

Wetlands may harbour species formerly more abundant when environmental conditions were different, known as 'relicts'. In the Ouse Washes of England, for example, there are relicts of the time when the sea flooded the area: sea aster (*Aster tripolium*), wild celery (*Apium graviolens*) and sea club-rush (*Scirpus maritimus*). Today the sea is 30 kilometres away. In the Pančićka Rašelina peat bog of East Bohemia and the peatlands of northern England and Scotland, cloudberry (*Rubus chamaemorus*) and *Sphagnum lindbergii* moss are relicts of a more extensive arctic-alpine community once covering much of northwest Europe.

Wetlands provide refuges for wild species even in highly industrialised centres. The dense shrub-scrub of the pocosin wetlands in North Carolina, one of the more industrialised southern US states, are refuges for the black bear, the white-tailed deer and the bobcat, together with the endangered (in North Carolina) eastern diamondback rattlesnake and alligator.

The Sundarbans forest of coastal India and Bangladesh is the largest remaining habitat of the renowned Royal Bengal tiger, which preys on the spotted deer. Deer and tiger are closely linked not only by the food chain, but also by environmental conditions which provide vital cover, shelter and space. The Sundarbans provide the last refuge in the region for a large number of other mammals, reptiles and amphibians, many of which are classified as endangered [77]. This and other wetlands are able to protect species not so much because they themselves are protected, but because they are among the last true wildernesses on earth, making them largely inaccessible to people. Tigers do not necessarily need wetlands, but they do need large stretches of wilderness, such as the Sundarbans.

The spotted deer in turn eat the leaves of a mangrove (*Sonneratia apetala*) and grasses. Fishing cats and mongooses live in and around the mangroves. Flying foxes roost in the mangroves of Australia, and proboscis monkeys are endemic in Borneo mangroves. The spotted cuscus (a marsupial) is common in the mangroves of Papua New Guinea. Throughout the world, mangrove birdlife is rich, and includes cormorants, herons, storks, pelicans, eagles, kites, ospreys, kingfishers and shorebirds. Crocodiles abound but are increasingly threatened or endangered over large parts of their range [78]. "Mangroves are far more than biological curiosities", notes Donald MacIntosh, an aquaculture adviser for the UK Overseas Development Administration (ODA); "they are intrinsic to the tropical coastal ecosystem currently containing large human populations" [79].

Wetland plants and animals are dependent not only on their environment but also on each other, through often complex food and nutrient cycles. In the Amazon, two crocodile species (*Melanosuchus niger* and *Caiman crocodylus*) feed mainly on fish. Yet when these predators were removed from some areas, there was a sharp decline in fish populations and in the catches of fishermen [80]. The predator's excreta was apparently a key element in the food chain, important to high fishery production.

In the Florida Everglades, alligators deepen and enlarge pools in the limestone — so-called 'gator-holes'. These pools attract fish, and in the dry season sustain not only large numbers of fish but the large numbers of fish-eating birds which congregate around the pools. In the Sundarbans, some birds visiting mangroves for nectar also remove plant-damaging insects. Without the birds, forest productivity would decline.

So it is important to maintain all species of wetland wildlife, so that their precise roles in the ecosystem can be fully determined. In many cases the very existence of other species, the productivity of economically important populations (such as fish, shellfish and grazing animals) and the well-being of human communities are at stake, quite apart from any scientific, cultural or recreational values associated with wildlife and the ecosystem.

Patrick Dugan/WWF

A caiman in the Pantanal, Brazil. Wetland plants and animals are linked in complex food and nutrient cycles. When two crocodile species (which feed mainly on fish) were removed from parts of the Amazon, there was a sharp decline in fish catches. Crocodile excreta was apparently a key element in the fisheries food chain.

Specialised plants

The fact that wetlands are permanently or periodically waterlogged has produced some extremely specialised adaptations among wetland plants.

Aquatic plants are porous and contain tissue with large intercellular spaces called 'aerenchyma'. Almost half the volume of rice roots growing in waterlogged soil may be air space, allowing growth in an oxygen-poor environment which would be lethal to terrestrial plants. Some trees, notably mangroves and the swamp cypress (*Taxodium distichum*), have evolved curious projections called 'knees' (pneumatophores) which develop from lateral roots near the surface and protrude sometimes more than 20 cm above the soil surface. The precise function of these organs has caused considerable scientific debate, but there is general agreement that they help plant roots to 'breathe'. The knees make for beautiful stands of trees, but they also have practical benefits by increasing sedimentation rates, so building up soil around the trees.

Most importantly, many species can cope with toxins produced in the soil under anaerobic (oxygen lacking) conditions. They can also convert nutrients into plant material without the benefit of oxygen, a chemical process which in some cases can result in the accumulation of significant quantities of ethanol.

The study of such species has both academic and economic motives. Studying the biochemical capabilities of wetland plants can aid scientists in understanding processes which may help them develop fermentation systems for the production of valuable chemicals. It can also help develop improved crop strains which might suffer occasional flooding. The list of wetland plants suitable for study and development is huge, but salt-loving plants give some idea of the potential.

Surviving salt and drought. The recent African famines have focused attention on the fragility of the world's dryland agricultural systems. Large tracts of the world's drought-stricken lands are saline and suffer from sand encroachment; between 400 and 950 million hectares are affected. Faulty irrigation has left much of the African drylands saline, and similarly has recently affected the vital food producing areas of the Murray Basin in Australia. In all, the UN Food and Agriculture Organization estimates that half the planet's irrigated land (120 million hectares) has suffered some reduction of crop yields due to salinisation [81].

Coastal wetlands offer science many examples of plants which have evolved to cope with sandy soils which are periodically very dry, as well as with salty conditions. These plants offer hope that such environments can be cropped successfully.

Professor James Aronson, Plant Introduction Officer at the Ben Gurion University of the Negev, Israel, holds that the lowly mangrove is a gene pool worthy of improvement, management and domestication. "The rule has been rather to exploit the hell out of them till they're gone, then look around for imported alternatives at triple the original cost", he notes in recent correspondence with the World Wildlife Fund [82]. Mangroves can be used for fodder, firewood, charcoal, tannin and medicines, and could be developed further as integrated coastal agroforestry production systems, where they are already growing. The timber and ornamental values under cultivated conditions are currently being investigated in Kenya, Egypt and Sudan.

Saltgrasses such as Palmers saltgrass (*Distichlis palmeri*), originally found in large areas of the Colorado delta and the Gulf of California, were formerly used as food by the Cocopa Indians. Related species, along with the very abundant cordgrass, may eventually yield 'cultivars' (cultivated varieties) for the production of fodder and silage. Seablites or saltworts (*Suaeda*) and glassworts (*Salicornia* spp.) produce edible seed oils high in protein and could play a large role in future seawater-based agricultural schemes. Nipa palm, characteristic of the mangrove forests of Asia and Oceania, is a versatile plant providing thatching material, medicines and fermented alcohol. The governments of Papua New Guinea and the Philippines are considering cultivating the sugar-producing Nipa palms on a large scale. They would use the sugar to make alcohol, and then mix the alcohol with petrol, saving money on oil imports — as the Brazilian government is doing with its programme to produce fuel alcohol from sugar cane.

Aronson has identified over 1,250 species of true 'salt-loving' plants (halophytes), many of which have potential for one or more economic uses, including fodder and forage, fuel for wood burners, ornaments for landscaping and land reclamation or stabilisation, breeding or genetic stock for crops, industrial products (gums, fibre, chemicals), and food.

Aronson believes that 32,000 km of desert coastlines, as well as large areas of interior deserts, could be brought under cultivation with the right species and management techniques. Already in the extremely salty Lake Texcoco, northeast of Mexico City, the saltgrass *Distichlis spicata* has been used to stabilise 6,000 hectares of lake bed, dramatically reducing dust storms. This planting has been incorporated into a scheme using sewerage water to irrigate the lake bed, producing cattle forage for much of the year. Increased use of halophytes in arid and semi-arid regions seems very likely in the future, both because of rapidly escalating desertification and salinisation and the difficulty of providing enough pure water to grow conventional crops in these areas [83].

This would reduce the pressure on freshwater wetlands increasingly threatened by farmers and their governments using this water for conventional agriculture and irrigation, with dubious economic benefits.

Animals — diverse but threatened

Countless invertebrates live in wetlands. Some are specific to particular wetlands (some even to single plant species) and are particularly sensitive to environmental disturbance such as pollution and habitat change [84]. Among dragonflies, the relict species *Epiophlebia laidlawi* in Nepal is disappearing fast due to cattle overgrazing the riverside vegetation. *Magalagnion pacificum* in the Hawaiian Islands is on the verge of extinction due to predation by the mosquito fish (*Gambusia*), introduced by man as a pest control measure [85].

Major river systems such as the Amazon, Zaire and Mekong can support 1,000 or more fish species [86]. Reptiles, amphibians, birds and mammals abound. Tropical estuaries, rivers and floodplains are habitats for dolphin, manatees and turtles such as the grey Central American river turtle (*Dermatemys mauvei*), heavily hunted and now listed as vulnerable in the *Red Data Book* of the International Union for Conservation of Nature and Natural Resources (IUCN).

Seven crocodile species are endangered worldwide, and a further three are listed as vulnerable in the *Red Data Book*. One of the most severely threatened is the Orinoco crocodile *Crocodylus intermedius*. Once the dominant carnivore in the Orinoco River basin, it has been reduced to a few hundred individuals by hunting in Colombia and Venezuela.

The endangered West African manatee (*Trichechus senegalensis*) is now restricted to a few strongholds in the coastal lagoons and mangroves of the Senegal River delta, and in the inner delta of the Niger. Populations of the Amazonian manatee *Trichechus inunguis* have yet to recover from commercial hunting between 1935 and 1954, when 400,000 skins of this curious plant-eating aquatic mammal were exported from Brazil. Areas like the 8,500 hectares of freshwater lagoons and swamp forest at Quero y Salado in Honduras are crucial for the existence of the Caribbean manatee (*Trichechus manatus*), the Amazon crocodile (*Crocodylus acutus*) and the Brown caiman (*Caiman crocodilus fuscus*).

Wetlands can support a rich mammal fauna. The complex of islands, mudflats and shallow seas of the Banc d'Arguin, Mauritania, supports Dorcas gazelle, jackal, sand fox (*Vulpes rueppelli*), sand cat (*Felis margarita*), weasel and hyena. Warthog are found in the Parc National des Oiseaux du Djoudj of the Senegal delta. The life cycles and migration patterns of many wild herbivores of the African floodplains are adapted to the wetland flooding regimes. In the Sudd of the Sudan the construction of the Jonglei Canal (see Chapter 8) may yet lead to the demise of the large 'tiang' antelope, reedbuck and Mongalla gazelle.

Other herbivores are more adjusted to life in standing water. The capybara feeds on grasses and aquatic plants in the floodplains and swamps of South America. The even more remarkable lechwe (*Kobus leche kafuensis*) of the Kafue Flats, Zambia, is able to graze while standing in water up to 50 cm deep. Its population has declined from 94,000 before the dam closure in 1972 in the Kafue Gorge [87] to 50,000 today [88], though some people consider poaching to be just as important a factor. Already classified as vulnerable, the species will survive only if its habitat, progressively reduced due to water control projects upstream, is preserved.

The marsh deer (*Blastocerus dichotomus*) is also well adapted to its wetland life in the southwest Mato Grosso in the Pantanal of Brazil. However, its numbers are diminishing rapidly due to poaching, to brucellosis transmitted by domestic livestock, and to habitat loss caused by the spread of ranching and agriculture.

Deer inhabit wetlands throughout Asia and North America. In the

Mark Boulton/ICCE

The Kafue lechwe is unique to the Kafue Flats of Zambia, where it thrives on the enriched bottomlands and floodplains exposed by falling floodwaters. But the building of the Kafue Gorge Dam in 1972 has helped nearly halve the number of lechwe.

Sundarbans, deer and wild pigs are important prey for the Bengal tiger. Habitat loss has already led to the disappearance of mammals like the Javan rhinoceros, wild water buffalo, swamp deer (*Cervus duvauceli*), and hog deer (*Axis porcinus*) from the Bangladesh basin [89]. The tiger, like other wetland cats (e.g. the jaguar of South America and the Sumatran tiger — now found only in Sumatra) requires a large contiguous habitat for survival. The Bengal tiger's reputation as a man-killer complicates conservation strategy. However, if the Sundarbans tiger population is reduced, the population of deer and pig will rise, and so too will the damage they do to forest production and thus to the livelihoods of those dependent on the mangroves.

Tropical wetlands host a valuable but threatened range of monkeys. The leaf monkey (*Presbytis cristata*) in Thailand and the proboscis monkey (*Nasalis larvatus*) in Borneo are both vulnerable species inhabiting mangroves. Sykes monkey, the Vervet monkey, the baboon, the Lesser Galago and the Zanzibar bushbaby are found in the floodplain forests of the lower Tana delta of Kenya, together with two endemic subspecies: the Tana River red colobus (*Colobus badius rufomitratus*) and the Tana River mangabey (*Cercocebus galeritus galeritus*). The Tana monkeys are classified as endangered and may disappear with future agricultural development of the delta.

Some wetland species — plant and animal — have recently become extinct: the mangrove *Bruguiera gymnorhiza* in Taiwan, the orchid *Schoenorchis perpusillus* in Singapore, the red wolf in Florida and the American crocodile in Venezuela. Extinction is an ever growing threat as the wetland habitat diminishes.

Waterfowl and other birds

Both coastal and inland wetlands are vital waterfowl habitats for year-round residents, but are also feeding, breeding, wintering and resting sites for millions of migratory birds. The flyways of many species are not just international but intercontinental. It was the importance of wetlands as habitat for waterfowl which spurred the first diplomatic efforts towards their preservation and the resulting Ramsar convention (see Chapter 7).

In August 1974, Australia became the first country to sign the convention, which regards wetlands as a resource "of great economic, cultural, scientific and recreational value" and recognised that waterfowl "should be regarded as an international resource". It was appropriate that Australia was first, for it plays host much of the year to such species as the Japanese snipe, curlew and sandpiper, which migrate as far as Japan and Siberia. Up to 26 migratory species use the Cairns mudflats in Queensland, including black swan, ibis, egret, chestnut teal, lotus bird and spur-winged plover.

Over 12 million duck nest and breed annually in the northern US wetlands, which — with the wet habitats of the Canadian prairies — host over 60% of the continent's breeding duck population. About 2.5 million of the three million mallards and nearly all the four million wood duck in the Mississippi flyway winter in the bottomland hardwood forests and marshes of the southern States.

Shorebirds are among the farthest migrating birds. Some sanderling (*Calidris alba*) breed in the wet tundra of Alaska, but winter in Argentina; the American golden plover (*Pluvialis dominica dominica*) also breeds on the tundra and migrates 20,000 km — via coastal Labrador, the Lesser Antilles and the northern coastal zone of South America — to winter in Argentina. It then returns along the wetlands of Central America, the Gulf of Mexico and the Mississippi flyway to the north.

Seven million shorebirds breeding in northern Europe and the Soviet Union winter along the Atlantic shores of Africa. The wetlands of the

Senegal delta are particularly important for migrants from the north because the area is one of the first places with permanent freshwater south of the Sahara. About three million migrants, mainly ducks and waders, use the area. Given the reduced water flows due to drought in the Sahel and increasing controls upstream, the Parc National des Oiseaux du Djoudj is the only significant zone of seasonal flooding remaining in the area. The wetland regime is vital not only to northern region species, such as garganey and shoveller, but also to a rich variety of African birds, such as the great white pelican, white-faced tree duck, and several species of egret.

Mauritania's Banc d'Arguin is one of the largest intertidal sandflats in the world. The fisheries provided 60% of the country's export earnings in 1984, reflecting the high productivity of a wetland complex internationally famous as the major African wintering site for northern shorebirds and an important breeding site for fish-eating species. About 30% of the Atlantic flyway shorebird migrants winter here, including 800,000 dunlin, 550,000 black-tailed godwits, several species of curlew and plover, and the increasingly threatened European spoonbill (*Platalea leucorodia*). Breeding species include 2,000 great white pelican, 1,500 grey heron, 3,000 greater flamingos and the endemic spoonbill (*Platalea leucorodia balsaci*).

Inland, as well as on the coast, the floodplain wetlands of the Sahel and other parts of Africa are important wintering and breeding areas. The inner delta of the Niger is especially important for migratory garganey and pintail, but numbers vary enormously due to the effects of drought. In 1978 there were 480,000 garganey, but in the drought year of 1984 only 148,000 were counted. Pintail declined in similar proportion. Nearly 400 bird species have been recorded in the Kafue Flats of Zambia, and over 400 in the Okavango delta of northwestern Botswana.

However, the importance of wetlands is not always related to numbers. Some are vital for rare or endemic species. At Bharatpur, the former Royal Game Reserve in Rajasthan, India, thousands of birds were once shot on a single day's hunting by a prince, viceroy or visiting general. The reserve now offers sanctuary to exotic migrants from Afghanistan and Tibet, bar headed geese from China, greylag geese from Siberia, and the rare Siberian cranes from the Arctic.

In Hawaii the endangered Hawaiian stilt, Hawaiian coot, Hawaiian gallinule and Hawaiian duck depend on wetlands for their survival. The Black River Lower Morass in Jamaica provides habitat for 102 out of the 227 bird species known in the country, and is a vital breeding area for the increasingly rare West Indian tree duck.

The small Acraq oasis, the only area of standing water in the Jordan desert, is a vital stepping stone for the enormous numbers of birds —

86

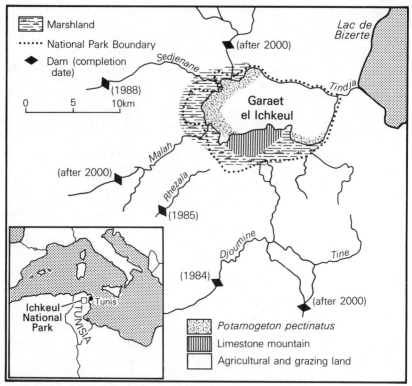

Garaet el Ichkeul, Tunisia.

including swallows, sandmartins, lesser whitethroats, wagtails, shorebirds and waterfowl — which migrate between the Red Sea, Asia Minor and southeast Europe across hostile desert terrain [90]. Many of the small wetland complexes of the Caribbean and Central America serve as similar stepping stones for migrating species from the North American Arctic.

The Camargue in France, the Marismas del Guadalquivir in Spain and Garaet el Ichkeul to the southwest of Bizerte in Tunisia are among the most important waterfowl sites in the world. Lake Ichkeul is one of the last of the once common freshwater lakes remaining along the coast of North Africa; almost all the rest have been drained. The lake — with extensive growth of the aquatic plant *Potamogeton* — and the surrounding marshes support 100,000-200,000 birds in winter (although 380,000 were recorded in 1973). Coot, wigeon, pochard and greylag goose come in large but varying numbers, depending in part on water levels. The recent plans to dam the principal wadis (seasonally dry river beds) feeding the lake represent a major threat to the wetland habitat, especially the growth of *Potamogeton* and waterfowl which depend on it [91].

The Wadden Sea is undoubtedly the most important single wetland in Western Europe, and of vital importance to huge numbers of waterfowl [92]. During the course of the year the number of birds per square kilometre in the Dutch Waddenzee averages one hundred times that in the middle of the North Sea and one thousand times that in the North Atlantic [93]. The region supports the largest population of avocets in the world. They nest here along with eider duck, sandwich tern and little tern, and the spoonbill (*Platalea leucorodia*), which arrives from its winter quarters in Africa — perhaps Senegal or Mauritius — in spring.

One of the largest concentrations of birds is around the island of Texel in the Netherlands, where the economic spin-off from the bird life can be measured at least in part from the volumes of visitors in spring and autumn. The purchase of a 40-hectare site in 1909 by the Netherlands Society for the Promotion of Nature Reserves was supported by the people of Texel and also by the ferry company linking the island to the mainland — the Texel Steamship Company. Windmills are still used, not to pump water out of the area but to keep water levels higher than the surrounding farmland. This maintains the marsh and reedbeds so important as bird habitat [94]. Among the Texel species are dunlin, godwits, knot, terns, gulls, ruffs, plovers, swans (mute, Bewick and whooper), mallard, teal, garganey, pintail, shovelers, tufted duck, warblers and buntings. It is not just the coastal wetlands that are important. At any one time, 10,000 whimbrels (*Numenius phaeopus*) roost on the Fochtelöer Fen, one of the last peat moors in the Netherlands; this is over 10% of the population migrating through Western Europe.

Even comparatively small peat bogs in the western islands of Scotland and in Ireland winter populations of the Greenland race of the white-fronted goose. On the island of Islay off the west coast of Scotland, the Duich Moss bog is the winter home for 600 white-fronted Greenland geese. Adjoining peat is already used by Scottish Malt Distillers to flavour the famous 'single malt' whisky produced on the island, an activity which provides essential employment in a community suffering from low incomes and high unemployment levels.

Plans to extend peat cutting into Duich Moss itself, authorised by the local planning committee and endorsed by the Secretary of State for Scotland, led to passionate arguments between local residents and conservationists. A public meeting on Islay in August 1985, saw the conservationists shouted down by local people concerned that failure to exploit the bog might result in the loss of jobs [95]. The bog is designated a site of special scientific interest, and a European Community directive has ordered protection of the geese habitat. But the conflict between local interests and those of the wider human community will inevitably increase, becoming more acrimonious and difficult to resolve as the natural resource is allowed to diminish.

Human interests, human values

Wetlands support agriculture and fisheries and are treasure troves of genetic resources. True. But it should not be forgotten that people — rapidly growing numbers of people — *like* wetlands and wetland plants and animals, something that is hard to quantify in financial terms.

In 1951, just over 30,000 tourists visited Texel (the Netherlands); today the figure is closer to 250,000. The area's natural landscape and birdlife are the major draw. It is near big urban populations, and these people have transportation and growing amounts of leisure time — factors which all make the wetland more valuable as recreation areas. But people travel longer distances to see the flamingos of the French Camargue, and nearly a million people annually visit the vast array of plant and animal life in the Florida Everglades. National waterfowl sanctuaries attract millions of visitors. In 1984, more than half a million people visited the seven Wildfowl Trust centres in Britain, and more than a third of a million people belong to Britain's Royal Society for the Protection of Birds.

In 1980, 28.8 million people in the United States (17% of the population) took special trips to observe, photograph or feed wildlife [96]. Wetlands figure prominently in these visits; they also offer various types of recreational hunting. In 1980, 5.3 million Americans spent $638 million on hunting waterfowl and migratory birds in the United States [97]. R.L. Johnston, principal silviculturist with the US Forest Service at Stoneville, Mississippi, maintains that there is probably no better game habitat in the US than southern bottomland forests. One 2,000-hectare tract of privately owned bottomland hardwoods located along the Mississippi River has had an annual average of 4,100 hunting parties. Average annual harvest for the past five years has been 221 deer, 140 turkeys and numerous squirrels, rabbits, racoons and ducks [97a].

Tidal and inland wetlands offer spectacular scenery. Many of the upland peatlands of Britain are within areas designated as national parks (but, unlike national parks in many other countries, large areas of British parks are settled or actively farmed). Land adjacent to the scenic saltmarshes of Cape Cod, Massachusetts, attracts prices of $100-150,000 per hectare — even higher closer to the urban fringes.

As transport and communications improve in developing countries, they may be able to take advantage of the tourist potential of wetland reserves. Already in Botswana, wildlife safaris are worth over $15 million annually. Tourism is the largest single employer in the town of Maun, on the edge of the Okavango delta. The potential earnings in foreign currency elsewhere are immense, and sustainable provided the wetland habitat and species are maintained. Such maintenance requires information and management. There are unparalleled opportunities for governments to earn tourist revenue from still relatively intact wetlands. Examples include Quero y Salado in Honduras, the coastal zone of Guinea-Bissau, Tortugeo in Costa Rica, the Banc D'Arguin in Mauritania, the Pantanal in Brazil and the Sundarbans in Bangladesh. Much, however, depends on political stability.

Some of the greatest potential is in Indonesia. Kalimantan and Irian Jaya have some of the world's largest, virtually undisturbed swamps, rich in plant and animal species. Yet the Indonesian government is trying to resettle millions of colonists from the crowded island of Java into the forests and swamps of Kalimantan (there are plans to settle 100,000 families in East Kalimantan) and Irian Jaya, habitats that often cannot support the type of intense agriculture these settlers bring with them. Already many settlements have failed, and are being supported on food aid. There is an urgent need to demonstrate not only the ecological values of the natural wetland resource, but also the economic arguments for their maintenance or non-destructive use, including wildlife and tourism.

The effects of increased pressure on Kalimantan have already been illustrated by the vegetation and subterranean peat fires which destroyed 3.5 million hectares in 1983-84. Described by IUCN as one of the worst environmental disasters of the century, primary tropical moist forest, peatlands and swamp were incinerated at a direct economic cost of $2-12 billion. The ecological cost was incalculable: large areas of the Kutai Nature Reserve and its rich wildlife of bears, leopards, pigs and civets were lost. While the unusually dry conditions of 1982 and 1983 (induced by a shift in the ocean current El Niño) increased flammability, the likelihood of severe fires was increased by logging, and forest clearance producing litter debris and shrub growth. Slash and burn peasant farming was probably the immediate cause of the fires, but their impact would have been much less had there been no increased commercial activity [98].

Chapter 7

The threatened landscape

According to some experts, the world may have lost half its wetlands since 1900 [99]. This could be an overstatement for the Third World, where we still have little idea of the full extent of wetlands, but it is no exaggeration for developed countries.

The United States alone has lost an estimated 54% (87 million hectares) of its original wetlands. From the 1950s to the 1970s, losses ran at 185,000 hectares per year — an area larger than the entire Panama Canal zone [100]. Agricultural development has been by far the largest single cause of loss, accounting for 87% of recent wetland losses in the contiguous United States. Urban development has taken 8% and other developments another 5% [101].

Until relatively recently, disease, flooding and waterlogged soils tended to keep large numbers of people and large development projects out of extensive wetland regions [102]. This has been particularly true in poorer nations, where traditional economies have continued to husband the wetland ecosystem rather than alter it. However, modern technology, foreign aid programmes and demands for new agricultural land and other resources have removed the natural immunity of large wetlands to economic 'development'. The location of wetlands along rivers, on coasts and on flat land with inherently fertile soils, has offered many motives for people to convert them to other uses.

The case of the inner delta of the Niger epitomises many of the worst problems facing wetlands. During the flood season, the fishery supports more than 10,000 families. During the dry season, the rich pasture of the floodplain supports more than a million head of cattle, and produces staple crops. Overgrazing, overfishing and plans to build flood control structures may permanently limit the extent of the pastureland and fisheries. Planned upstream dams — as far inland as Guinea — could have a major effect not only on the inner delta but on the outer coastal delta, 2,500 km away in Nigeria.

Pollution poses further threats. In Pakistan, pollution and disturbance from agro-chemicals factories, a steel mill and the construction of a new port at Karachi pose a serious threat to the estuaries of the Indus delta. Two creeks alone produce more than 800 tonnes of prawns annually, providing a major source of foreign exchange. In Central America,

J. LaTourette/WWF

A new housing development in the mangroves of Florida. The United States has lost more than half its original wetlands (an area almost as big as Nigeria). Agricultural development and urban development are the major causes of loss.

pesticide contamination is a major problem in almost all the coastal wetlands bordering banana, oil palm, cotton and rice plantations.

There are also natural threats, such as climatic changes. The Sahelian droughts are extreme examples, but even in temperate areas the natural environment can take its toll. Bird surveys in the Somerset wetlands of England indicate that breeding waders and other wetland birds declined by up to 50% in many sites during 1983-85. Peter Nicholson, regional officer of the Nature Conservancy Council, believes this was not the result of any changes in farming in that time, but "the accumulative result of several dry years and poor breeding success" [103].

The Ramsar convention

The wetland issue is fast becoming one of the most contentious and

HUMAN THREATS

Direct

Drainage for crop production, timber production and mosquito control.

Dredging and stream channellisation for navigation channels, flood protection, coastal housing developments, and reservoir maintenance.

Filling for dredged spoil and other solid waste disposal, roads and highways, and commercial, residential and industrial development.

Construction of dykes, dams, levees and seawalls for flood control, water supply, irrigation and storm protection.

Discharges of materials (e.g. pesticides, herbicides, other pollutants, nutrient loading from domestic sewage and agricultural runoff, and sediments from dredging and filling, agricultural and other land development) into waters and wetlands.

Mining of wetland soils for peat, coal, sand, gravel, phosphate and other materials.

Indirect

Sediment diversion by dams, deep channels and other structures.

Hydrological alterations by canals, spoil banks, roads and other structures.

Subsidence due to extraction of groundwater, oil, gas, sulphur and other minerals.

NATURAL THREATS

Subsidence (including natural rise of sea level), droughts, hurricanes and other storms, erosion, and biotic effects.

Major causes of wetland loss and degradation. Sources: Tiner et al, after Zinn & Copeland 1982 and Gosselink & Baumann 1980.

politically sensitive questions facing environmental scientists. The future of wetlands seems to rest much more with the outcome of political and legal debate and patterns of economic and social development rather than with any natural processes.

Governments need to be convinced that they have an obligation to maintain and preserve wetlands. This is especially urgent given that functions such as food chain support and wildlife maintenance often extend well beyond natural frontiers, and sometimes across continents. But the necessary national legislation is virtually non-existent, and is usually unenforceable anyway, given the limited resources, and political regimes and attitudes of many countries.

The protection of wetlands in Europe is being tightened, but the pace of change is slow, and handicapped by entrenched opposition to regulation, and hard pressed legislative timetables. In the United States there has been a more concerted effort to give wetlands legal protection. The work of American lawyer Jon Kusler, author of *Strengthening State Wetland Regulations* (US Fish and Wildlife Service 1980) and *Our National Wetland Heritage — A Protection Guidebook* (Environmental Law Institute, 1983), underlines the trend. The latter text gives legal and procedural guidelines to help administrators develop more responsible attitudes towards wetlands.

Kusler recommends that local government protects wetlands through a general wetland protection policy designed to protect wetland functions important to the community. This policy should require that anyone wanting to alter or develop wetland areas should have to prove that the proposed activities could not be located at upland sites. "If activities are conducted in wetlands," Kusler suggests, "measures should be taken to minimise the impact upon wetland functions". He also recommends — *inter alia* — educating the public on the values, hazards, and threats to wetlands; acquiring where possible wetlands that need total protection; regulating wetland activities; reducing property tax assessments to reflect wetland land use restrictions; and initiating efforts to restore damaged or destroyed natural wetland vegetation and hydrological regimes.

At the global level, the need for wetland protection picked up momentum in the early 1960s. The International Biological Programme took a lead with Project AQUA and IUCN with Project MAR, designed to increase awareness of the importance of these ecosystems and the threats to which they were increasingly exposed. A series of conferences and technical meetings, held mainly under the auspices of the International Wildfowl Research Bureau (based at Slimbridge, England), culminated in the Convention on Wetlands of International Importance, Especially as Waterfowl Habitat, known more simply as the Ramsar convention after the Iranian town where it was opened on 2

February 1971. The convention came into force on 21 December 1975, four months after the seventh state had ratified.

Wetlands are the only particular ecosystem type to have their own international convention. The main aim of the convention is to halt the decline of wetland habitats, and maintain their ecological functions and wildlife. Contracting countries agree to include wetland conservation in national planning, to promote sound utilisation of wetlands, to create properly wardened nature reserves, and to develop management research and training facilities. Every country must designate at least one wetland for inclusion in the List of Wetlands of International Importance. The list is maintained by IUCN in its capacity as 'Bureau' under the convention. As of October 1985, the list included 323 wetland sites, covering more than 20 million hectares. New areas are being added annually.

Three meetings of contracting parties have been held:

* a technical meeting in Cagliari, Italy, in November 1980, when members pledged to make special efforts to help developing countries join the convention;
* an extraordinary meeting in Paris in December 1982, when a protocol was adopted which redressed two technical problems: the lack of an amendment clause, and the lack of language versions of the convention, which had been a barrier to France and other francophone countries signing;
* a meeting in May 1984 in Groningen, the Netherlands, when a great deal of time was spent discussing the problems of reconciling nature conservation and economic development in developing countries, and how financial support could be given to the poorer nations of the world for conservation.

On the plus side, the convention is a first step towards placing international obligations on the land management decisions of sovereign countries. There has been no delisting of a Ramsar site, even though this is permitted in circumstances of "urgent national interest". As David Navid, Head of IUCN's International Relations Unit (which manages the convention) says, "designation has been proven to be a potent conservation tool" [104].

But the convention has its problems:

* Obligations on the signatories are maintained by persuasion, cooperation and moral pressure, rather than by legal constraints.
* Some countries are reluctant to list more than one or just a few of their wetlands, even though they may have more that are important.

* The convention is often criticised for having too few non-European members; there are large parts of the world — particularly Africa south of the Sahara, Latin America and southeast Asia — where few or no countries are signatories. (Of the 38 signatories in December 1985, 21 were European and only 13 were from the Third World.*
* Progress is hampered by lack of finance. If IUCN and the International Waterfowl Research Bureau (IWRB — which provides the scientific advice) did not meet the costs of administration, the convention could not work at all. Neither organisation has the money itself to expand the work under the convention.
* The convention has no permanent secretariat.

Occasional conferences of the Contracting Parties have tackled the more detailed technical deficiencies: at Groningen a task force was set up (consisting of representatives from Canada, Denmark, the Netherlands, Poland, Senegal, Sweden and Tunisia) to report to the next meeting in 1987 in Regina, Canada) on alternatives for a secretariat structure. But Regina must also attempt to give the convention a much sounder footing.

Drainage and flood control

"For centuries," notes David Baldock, director of Britain's Earth Resources Research Ltd, "the drainage of wetlands has been seen as a progressive, public spirited endeavour" [105].

One such 'progressive improvement' is flood control. About half of the Netherlands, once part of the complex delta of the Rhine, Meuse, Ems and Scheldt rivers, would be inundated at least periodically were it not for the array of dams, dykes and drainage networks built since the 8th Century. Today, 22% of Dutch agricultural land has artificial subsurface drainage [106], and new drainage is spreading at about 25,000 hectares per year [107].

Floods have encouraged drainage schemes that have led to wetland losses. Following successive severe floods, from the Middle Ages until

---

*Contracting parties at December 1985: Algeria, Australia, Austria, Bulgaria, Canada, Chile, Denmark, Federal Republic of Germany, Finland, German Democratic Republic, Greece, Hungary, Iceland, India, Iran, Ireland, Italy, Japan, Jordan, Mauritania, Morocco, the Netherlands, New Zealand, Norway, Pakistan, Poland, Portugal, Senegal, South Africa, Spain, Surinam, Sweden, Switzerland, Tunisia, UK, Uruguay, USSR and Yugoslavia. (The US has signed but not ratified. Preliminary documentation has also been lodged by Belgium, Mali, Egypt and Mexico, and France has ratified the protocol.)

Excavating a wetland stream in southwestern England. For centuries, the drainage of wetlands has been seen as a progressive, public-spirited endeavour. The area of fen, marsh and wet meadow in Britain has fallen steadily as wetland becomes farmland.

1947, many new engineering works were commissioned in the Fens of eastern England to increase the extent and depth of drainage control. Inevitably, the area of natural fen, marsh and wet meadow continued to decline and to be replaced by more arable acreage. But the land has continued to sink as peat has dried out, compacted, oxidised and eroded; this sinking has required more — and increasingly expensive — control measures.

As Europeans moved to the United States and colonised low-lying coastal and floodplain environments, they sought protection from floods. This led in turn to swamp drainage. The swamplands were originally owned by the federal government, and petitions to Congress were eventually brought for compensation for improvements undertaken by states. The resulting legislation — the Federal Swamp Land Acts of 1849-50 and 1860 — was intended not only to alleviate flood dangers, but to improve sanitation and reclaim land for agriculture. But large-scale flooding remained a problem in the lower Mississippi, spurring the building of levees and the setting aside of the Atchafalaya Swamp west of New Orleans as a floodbasin to divert

A natural channel in the Florida Everglades. Water is the keystone to the Everglades ecosystem. Flood control and changes in the volume and timing of water flow have led to declining numbers of birds, fish and crustaceans, changes in salinity, and invasion by exotic plant species.

excessive discharges away from New Orleans [108].

The 'flood protection' increasingly provided from state and federal money has been a major factor in the enormous loss of US wetlands since the mid-1800s. Average national losses for the US hide much greater regional losses. Most Florida developers and politicians have been trying to drain the Everglades and turn it over to farmland since the annexation of Florida to the United States in 1821. Severe floods in 1928, 1947 and 1948 resulted in the Central and South Florida Flood Control Project, which built or rebuilt almost 1,300 km of levees and 800 km of canals. Some 16,200 hectares of wetland were lost directly through the channel digging, and an additional 40,500 hectares were drained.

Flood control inevitably encouraged urban and agricultural expansion. Furthermore, 'flood control' in Florida severely disrupted the natural flood cycle and water regime of the Everglades National Park. The flow of water from Lake Okeechobee had long been affected by development, but further regulation and the building of a new levee completely blocked water flow into the Park in 1963 [109]. Despite

State or region	Original wetlands	Remaining wetlands	% loss	Date
Iowa — natural marshes	930,000	10,700	99	1981
California	2 million	182,000	91	1977
Nebraska — rainwater basin	38,000	3,400	91	1982
Mississippi alluvial plain	9.7 million	2.1 million	78	1979
Michigan	4.5 million	1.3 million	71	1982
North Dakota	2 million	810,000	60	1983
Minnesota	7.45 million	3.5 million	53	1981
Louisiana — forested wetlands	4.57 million	2.3 million	50	1980
Connecticut — coastal marshes	12,000	6,000	50	1982
North Carolina — pocosins	1 million	610,000	40	1981
South Dakota	810,000	525,000	35	1983
Wisconsin	4 million	2.7 million	32	1976

Wetland losses in selected US states and regions (numerous sources, data compiled in Tiner 1984).

agreement by the Army Corps of Engineers to maintain minimum water levels, water has frequently been too little, and in the wrong place at the wrong time to meet the needs of the natural biological system.

"Water is the keystone of the Everglades ecosystem", observes John Morehead, superintendent of the national park. Changes in the volume and timing of water flow have led to declining populations of several species of birds, declining fish and crustacean populations, changes in bay and estuarine salinity, and invasion by exotic plant species [110]. The pressures on what remains of the Everglades ecosystem, now largely contained within the national park boundaries, increased dramatically in the 1970s, reaching crisis level in the 1980s. The causes: increasingly uncertain water supplies controlled by the Army Corps of Engineers, expanding farmland and cities demanding more water and reducing water quality, and the threat of new development in the undeveloped East Everglades wetland.

Morehead and his colleagues in the National Park Service have had to fight hard to ensure the survival of the natural ecosystems. For the time

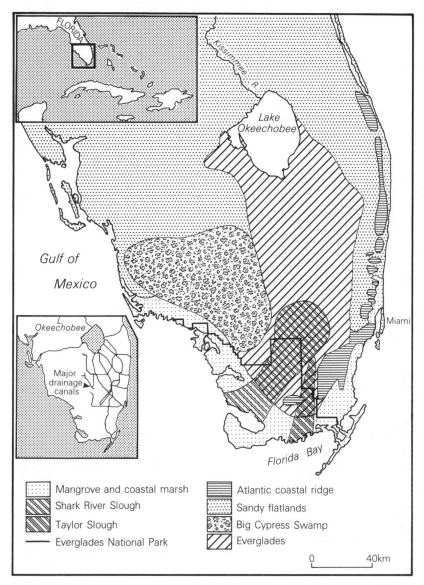

Gulf of

Mexico

Lake
Okeechobee

Kissimmee R.

Miami

Florida Bay

Okeechobee

Major
drainage
canals

FLORIDA

:::::: Mangrove and coastal marsh
Shark River Slough
Taylor Slough
—— Everglades National Park

Atlantic coastal ridge
Sandy flatlands
Big Cypress Swamp
Everglades

0   40km

The past and present extent of wetlands in the Florida Everglades.

State or region	Loss rate (ha/year)	Date
Lower Mississippi alluvial plain	66,000	1979
Louisiana — forested wetlands	35,300	1980
North Carolina — pocosins	17,600	1981
Prairie pothole region	13,400	1969
Louisiana — coastal marshes	10,000	1982
Great Lakes Basin	8,100	1981
Wisconsin	8,100	1976
Michigan	2,600	1981
Kentucky	1,450	1983
New Jersey — coastal marshes	1,250	1973
Palm Beach County, Florida	1,240	1982
Maryland — coastal wetlands	405	1983
New York — estuarine marshes	300	1972
Delaware — coastal marshes	180	1983

Examples of recent wetland loss rates in the US.

Agriculture	87%
Urban development	8%
Other development	5%

Causes of wetland losses in the conterminous United States — approx. 1955-1975.

being, they have succeeded; the Everglades are relatively safe. In 1983, the Florida state government launched a multi-million dollar 'Save our Everglades' project, emphasising the need for cooperation between the state and federal governments to guarantee the water regime needed to maintain the Everglades wetlands [111].

One aspect of the new approach is a two-year trial, begun in June 1985, of water delivery to the park based in part on actual recorded rainfall. This information is fed into a computer model, and the gates controlling water flow into the park are accordingly adjusted weekly.

There is no certainty, however, that this will provide permanent security; one of the urgent tasks currently facing Dr Gary Hendrix, director of the park's research division, is to collect enough data to help scientists and managers understand better how the ecosystem works, how precisely it reacts to external pressures and how management strategies can be developed or modified to maintain ecological diversity and integrity.

A recent study has found that nitrogen levels of less than 10% of agreed standards, and phosphorus content at the water quality standard agreed for water flowing into the park can speed up the decomposition of organic matter. It is impossible to predict all the implications of this finding, but already there have been changes in vegetation downstream of experimental channels due to the added nutrients [112]. This suggests that efforts to resist further agricultural expansion around the park and prevent fertiliser runoff reaching the wetlands must continue. It also suggests the need for wetland buffers wide enough to absorb existing and future increases.

In the mid-1970s, a major drainage and flood control scheme began to change the ecology of Jamaica's Black River Upper Morass, one of the key remaining wetland complexes in the Caribbean. The Black River Upper Morass Development Company (BRUMDEC), a subsidiary of the National Investment Bank of Jamaica and financed partly by a loan from the Inter-American Development Bank, has now 'reclaimed' some 2,000 hectares, mainly of peat, for agriculture. About 400 hectares is under rice cultivation, both for the local market and for potential export markets. Predictably, the dried peat has subsided, increasing the costs and difficulty of water management.

But more important still is the serious impact the scheme is having on the Lower Morass, a complex area of swamp forest, seasonally flooded grassland, freshwater marshes and, at the coast, shallow brackish lagoons, tidal marshes and mangroves. The swamp forest is a specialised community of major ecological importance, containing rare and endemic species; it is an obvious target for conservation.

Up to a thousand people may use the wetland for fishing and shrimping; for many it is the only means of livelihood. The area is an important breeding area for many waterfowl and the last stronghold of several species in Jamaica. It is a vital habitat for the declining population of American crocodile and for the few manatees which have escaped hunting. The wetlands are also an important breeding ground and nursery for commercially important fish and shrimp [113]. The shrimp catch alone is worth $1.5 million a year [113a].

This complex, highly integrated system is threatened. First, BRUMDEC has built dykes which speed sediment, once deposited in the upper basin, into the lower wetlands. Second, high levels of fertilisers, pesticides and other pollutants run off from the agricultural areas. Third, as the peat dries, it itself releases nutrients adding to the wetland load.

But just how far this has affected the wetland and its commercial 'services' (e.g. fisheries) has not been evaluated fully. The Petroleum Corporation of Jamaica has plans for more detailed monitoring. The number and size of shrimp appear to be decreasing, but the relative effect of agricultural development compared to other factors, such as overfishing, is impossible to gauge. Much of the existing environmental information on the wetland ecosystem of the Black River Morass comes from surveys carried out in connection with a proposed 'peat for energy' programme (see Chapter 9). If this controversial programme gets government approval, it also will drastically alter the Morass ecosystem — creating new open water bodies, establishing new flooding patterns and spawning ecological changes. We can only guess at the likely effect of these changes.

In Argentina, ecologist Manuel Nores identifies the most serious threats to wetlands as those arising from the building of dykes which divert water supplies and cause the drying out of swamps and marshes such as at the Bañados de Figueroa in Santiago del Estero and at the Bañados de la Amarga in Cordoba.

The Esteros del Ibera, a vast complex of over 10,000 sq km of shallow freshwater lakes, swamps with slow-moving water and extensive floating vegetation, seasonal marshes and wet grassland, is one of the most important wetlands in the country. Its large population of waterfowl includes abundant rails and tree ducks. It has the most important population left in Argentina of the swamp deer (*Blastocerus dichotomus*); caimans also flourish. It is threatened by proposed hydroelectric and irrigation dams along the Paraná River. There is also a proposal to prevent flooding from the Paraná by channelling excess water to the Esteros, creating a single large lake, but eliminating the majority of diverse wetland habitats [114].

Agricultural development:
Third World conflicts and dilemmas

Many of the world's remaining wetlands are in poor countries, or in the poorer regions of rich countries. They have survived because they are in places which have discouraged development, agricultural or otherwise. But these wetlands are now becoming increasingly attractive options for agricultural expansion and intensification in developing and often hungry countries.

The expansion of rice cultivation into the Rewa River delta on Viti Levu, Fiji, and into the mangroves of Guinea Bissau are examples of recent attempts to increase domestic food production in countries where most other flat land is already fully used. The decisions to alter these areas have not fully accounted for the loss of wetland functions the changes would cause; it may never be possible to evaluate the losses in fisheries productivity and water controls.

The urgent need to feed people is a very convincing argument, but it tends to treat the goal of local increases in food production in isolation. Draining wetlands may increase local yields over the short term, but may cause large reductions in yields elsewhere in the ecosystem, or reduce the entire ecosystem's ability to sustain harvests over the longer term. One cause of the 50% cut in the fish catch in the Grand Lac of the Mekong could be the clearance of trees for farming around the lake, in turn causing increased erosion, siltation and water cloudiness [115]. The hunger for agricultural land can lead to tragedy: the fertile new delta islands of the Ganges draw Bangladeshi fishermen and landless farmers; some 10,000 lost their lives on this land in the cyclone of May 1985.

Development plans for the Mekong basin and for the river floodplains and deltas of Africa and South America are proceeding fast. These schemes rarely consider fisheries losses (often far removed from the point of impact), reductions in wildlife and habitat, and reductions in water quality and the many other environmental properties controlled by wetlands. Or if they do, the considerations are usually overriden by short-term and more easily quantifiable economic arguments.

In most river basins, decisions in one country can have implications for the economy of others downstream. Plans for dam construction on the headwaters of the Niger River in Guinea may improve local agricultural production, but the ensuing changes in river flow rates may compromise not only the livelihoods of hundreds of thousands of people in Mali and Niger, who depend on the river flood for their survival, but also the fisheries of the Niger delta in Nigeria. If the vast wetland resources of Third World rivers are to make their full contribution to sustainable development, these and other conflicts must be resolved.

More and more flood control schemes are being incorporated into Third World development projects. These may be necessary where an aim of the project is to introduce more intensive agriculture. But in many cases, like the Tana delta project in Kenya and the building of embankments on parts of the Logone River in Cameroon, the losses of wetland functions must be weighed against the benefits of flood alleviation. In many such projects, the value of undisturbed, or little disturbed, wetlands are not given a realistic value in the equations.

There is ever-growing pressure to convert the mires of Africa, South America and southeast Asia to farmland. Indonesia has an estimated 17 million hectares of peatland, Malaysia 2.5 million, and Brazil 1.5 million [116]. Malaysia's commercial production of pineapples for the canning industry is already based almost exclusively on peat, which is frequently burnt to increase nutrient levels. Plans are well advanced to drain large peat areas in Brazil and Indonesia for agriculture [117].

Nearly a fifth of the wetlands identified as internationally important in Central and South America are threatened by direct drainage for farming or ranching [118]. But for the Third World as a whole, there is little certainty about rates of wetland loss or about the overall proportion threatened by agricultural development. Inventories of wetland resources, their ecological importance and their present economic significance are essential if their use, management and conservation is to be effectively planned.

The danger of acidified soils

Under certain conditions, pyrite (FeS_2) has been formed in clayey sediments deposited under brackish or saline conditions. When these sediments — known as potential acid sulphate (PAS) materials — are oxidised (for example by drainage), acid sulphate soils (ASS) develop, containing sulphuric acid and yellow jarosite. PAS materials are found in complex wet environments, including mangrove forests. They are difficult to exploit, and the consequences of using them carelessly are serious: when they turn acid they disrupt the natural system and adjacent croplands or aquaculture. They have poor levels of base saturation, contain aluminium and iron (which are especially toxic to rice and fish), and are low in phosphorus and nitrogen.

PAS materials are common — and acid sulphate soils have been formed — in the Mekong River and Saigon River deltas. The FeS_2 deposits are the result of a combination of iron-rich sediment, sulphates from sea water (reduced to sulphides by anaerobic conditions), organic matter from mangroves, tidal movement allowing the partial oxidation of sulphide to elemental sulphur (necessary for the formation of pyrite), chemically reducing bacteria and slow sedimentation rates [119]. Only melaleuca trees, some kinds of rushes, and other very acid-tolerant plants can survive in these soils, and birds and fish are scarce.

In Senegal, Sierra Leone and the Netherlands, the intensive, sudden drainage and aeration of PAS materials has been disastrous; reclamation of the acid sulphate soils formed has been possible only with hugely expensive chemical treatment, such as lime application. Only the maintenance of a high water table on acid sulphate soils (to prevent further pyrite oxidation and to reverse the process) has proved successful. The Vietnamese government has nonetheless given high priority since 1975 to the agricultural development of PAS areas, motivated in part by the apparently ideal flat land and abundant water resources.

The difficulty of developing acid sulphate soils for agriculture is illustrated by attempts to establish paddy in the soils supporting melaleuca forest that was defoliated during the Vietnam war (more than 90% of the melaleuca forest in the Mekong delta was affected). The enormous (more than a million hectares) backswamps of the delta consist entirely of acid sulphate soils in various stages of development; the swamps are inundated by the rivers in the wet season and dry up in the dry season. The area was originally half covered by melaleuca (the only tree that can stand the acids, but *not* a mangrove species) and half covered by reeds. Where paddy was established, the soils rapidly turned acid; the paddies had to be abandoned after just one or two seasons. Renewed oxidation of FeS_2 made recovery of the natural vegetation impossible. Not only was the rice farming a failure but the wildlife declined and a valuable breeding area for fish and shrimp was destroyed.

Apparently undeterred, Vietnam is still keen to develop the PAS areas of the Mekong delta. A major thrust of current work is the establishment of pilot schemes, costing nearly $3 million, to show how acid sulphate soils can be successfully used. At pilot farms in the Plain of Reeds and the Thanh Tri areas (in the Mekong delta), there are plans to develop new and improved techniques for cultivating the soils — as a showcase in a proposed worldwide UNEP system of pilot and demonstration projects in rational water resource management, and as a means of working out ways of making optimum use of the delta.

Professor Leendert Pons of the Agricultural University, Wageningen, the Netherlands, a leading authority on acid sulphate soils is eager to promote the replanting of melaleuca trees and the use of land for forestry rather than risking the possible serious ecological consequences of drainage and agriculture.

The consequences of misusing PAS land were tragically emphasised by events in the Orinoco delta of Venezuela in the late 1970s. Drainage and the construction of dams in the area brought about the formation of acid sulphate soils on lands inhabited by the Guaraunous Indians. Fields used to grow bananas and cassava were lost, and the reduction of vegetation affected wildlife, and so removed the major source of meat for local people. The Indians moved to another area, where a series of floods in 1976-80 claimed the lives of most of the population of 4-5,000. Very few survived; those that did are now classified as displaced persons [120].

Soybeans and timber:
market demands and pressures

Demand for soybeans and timber have been major factors in US wetland loss. Between 1959 and 1964, 400,000 hectares in the Mississippi delta region were drained and cleared almost exclusively for soybean; single tracts up to 20,000 hectares were bulldozed. In North Louisiana alone forested wetlands disappeared at a rate of 45,000 hectares a year. Louisiana's forested wetlands still disappear at the rate of 1.3% annually.

The economies of clearance and drainage were given a strange twist in the early 1970s by events off the Pacific coast of South America. Years of uncontrolled overfishing, suddenly compounded in 1972 by a change in the upwelling pattern of the cold, nutrient-rich current off the coast of Peru, brought a sudden collapse of the anchovy industry. As the largest source of protein meal collapsed, the demand for soybean increased and prices soared. Despite the huge costs of turning swampland into farmland in the United States (approximately $3,000/hectare in 1980 [121]), the anchovy crash made the cultivation of some of the most difficult wetland terrain very attractive.

Between 1973 and 1975, almost 202,000 hectares of wetlands on the coastal plain of North Carolina were cleared. Enormous agricultural corporations with substantial external investment moved into this development business in a big way. Companies such as First Colony Farms and Open Grounds Farm Inc. make up a very significant element of the 21% of pocosins controlled by corporate agriculture. Open Grounds Farm Inc. started clearing in 1974, and by 1977 8,000 hectares of pocosins had been converted to farmland [122].

As a result of this massive conversion to farmland, freshwater runoff increased, salinity was reduced, and nitrogen concentrations raised. The wetlands had provided a buffer against such occurrences; the farmland could not, and it was predicted that by the mid-1980s, the intensity and frequency of freshwater floods would reduce numbers of juvenile shrimp and fish [123].

The pocosins once covered nearly a million hectares of North Carolina. In 1980, only 281,000 hectares remained. Where once evaporation and transpiration from the wetlands and their plants was the major water output, today runoff predominates. There has been a dramatic reduction in habitat for rare and endangered plants and animals, along with a dramatic increase in the market value of these lands [124].

Growing national and international demands for timber and wood products have changed the character of most of the forested wetlands of the United States. Most of the virgin stands of bald cypress (*Taxodium distichum*) in the southern United States were logged after the Civil War of the 1860s. The lumber industry grabbed millions of hectares of federal land through bargain purchases and in some areas through construction grants for railways, canals and settlement. The onslaught was particularly great in Florida and Louisiana.

In 1869, the New York and Florida Lumber Land and Improvement Company was promised 445,000 hectares at 25 cents per hectare on the condition that it settled one new inhabitant for each 130 hectares received from the state of Florida [125]. Huge fortunes were made; corruption and accusations of fraud were rife, and there was no replanting. In Louisiana, vigorous cutting by the cypress industry

Edward Maltby

Pocosin swamps once covered nearly a million hectares of North Carolina in the United States. By 1981, just over a quarter remained. Massive clearance for farmland has increased the freshwater runoff (increasing the risk of floods), reduced salinity, and raised nitrogen levels.

between 1880 and 1925 caused pristine cypress strands to be replaced by second growth dominated by water tupelo trees (*Nyssa aquatica*) and maple (*Acer rubrum* var. *drummondii*), trees of much lower commercial value [126]. The removal of cypress and Atlantic white cedar (*Chamaecyparis thyoides*) in North Carolina had so depleted these species by the end of the 19th Century that pond pine and evergreen shrubs became the dominant species on the pocosins.

During the 1930s, the cheap pocosin land and second growth pine attracted pulp and paper companies which carried on the massive destruction of wetlands. Today big timber companies own about 44% of the pocosin land in North Carolina [127]. Much of this has been converted into drained, cultivated and fertilised pine plantation. Fertiliser application can increase pine productivity up to three times. With soaring world prices for wood products and returns exceeding $5,000 per hectare [128], this process — drain, cultivate, fertilise — will accelerate. The pressure on remaining pocosins and nearby estuaries will grow, almost certainly unchecked by ineffective legislation.

108

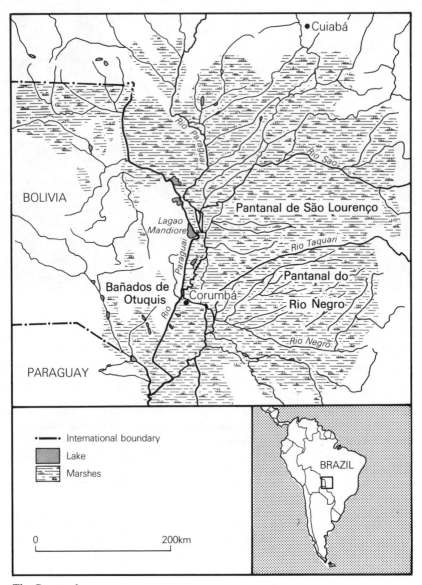

The Pantanal.

Poaching and drugs

Many Third World wetlands are large and remote. Traditional laissez-faire attitudes, the lack of effective law enforcement agencies, and the spread of the most extensive wetlands across international boundaries have made it difficult to legislate to control their use. The problem is illustrated by the vast Pantanal floodplain — 13 million hectares of marshland and seasonally inundated savanna, mainly in Brazil but bordering on Paraguay and Bolivia.

The region is a major illegal wildlife trafficking and cocaine smuggling centre. One species, the yacare caiman (*Caiman crocodilus yacare*), is particularly threatened; an estimated one million are poached each year [129] and the skins flown out illicitly to Paraguay or Bolivia. Payment may be in cocaine, which is then marketed throughout Brazil. Poachers may get up to $3 a skin, an attractive income, especially when high water levels in the Pantanal restricts ranch employment. To the reptile-skin industry in Europe, Japan and the United States the harvest is worth at least $120 million a year.

"In a region as vast and remote as the Pantanal," notes photojournalist Randall Hyman, "the law of the gun often prevails over the law of a distant government" [130]. Police enforcement is expensive — an 18 day operation in 1983 cost $150,000. But the impact of such intensive poaching is serious; the caimans have been exterminated from some areas, and the ecosystem has been upset. One indication of this has been the uncontrolled increase in piranhas.

The problems of the Pantanal do not stop at illegal hunting. Deforestation is bringing increased river turbidity and siltation; irrigation projects and hydroelectric dams are changing the hydrology; agricultural expansion threatens water quality and wildlife through nutrient and pesticide runoff; and industrial developments (particularly sugar cane processing and alcohol production) are likely to bring severe pollution problems [131].

Ferreira dos Santos, now chief of operations at the Brazilian state game commission, petitioned successfully for the Pantanal to be designated a 'national treasure'. But it is much more than this; it is an ecosystem of global importance and certainly the most important wetland in South America in terms of waterfowl populations. The waterfowl include huge numbers of resident birds, both on open water marsh and wet savanna. The Pantanal is also an essential staging post for Arctic shorebirds en route to and from wintering grounds in the south. Reduced flows and/or altered timings of floods would seriously affect an important fishery and reduce the habitat available for plants, birds, and the rich mammal and reptile fauna (including the caimans) already under pressure from illegal hunting.

Only 149,000 hectares of the Pantanal are protected (at least theoretically). The Brazilian government has earmarked $2.5 million for 'Operation Pantanal', an attempt to use economic strategies to save the wetland and its wildlife. The region has enormous tourist potential, which might relieve the poverty of some communities. Commercial caiman farming may well reduce the destruction of the wild population.

But the government will have to take on many other development interests with considerable political influence if wetland values and functions are to be maintained in the floodplain. The money for Operation Pantanal is not yet available. Randall Hyman, who interviewed many of the local inhabitants in the region in 1984, questions the seriousness of the country's commitment. "Plagued by staggering foreign debts, 200% annual inflation and steadily increasing poverty, Brazil may have its attention diverted from ecological issues for quite a while", he warns. Brazil, like many Third World nations, is not a signatory of the Ramsar convention. In circumstances like these the international community must exert the influence and find the necessary financial resources.

The problems posed by illegal operations in wetlands are not unique to Brazil. Jamaica's Negril Morass has suffered considerably in recent years from the illegal cultivation of marijuana. About half the swamp forest present in 1960 has been destroyed and much of the loss since 1978 is attributed to cannabis cultivation. Drainage, clearing and burning of vegetation has caused significant damage to the wetland complex. The debris of light aircraft in the Morass testify to the hazardous nature of moving the drug illicitly from such a remote location.

Hence the very remoteness and wilderness of wetlands poses conservationists with a dilemma. Increasing development and population and the inevitable strengthening of law enforcement may reduce the incidence and damage of illegal activity, but the developments themselves — such as farming and industrial activity in the Pantanal — may have a far more serious and permanent effect on the ecosystem. To protect wild wetlands might be regarded as condoning illicit activities. It is a risk, though, that environmentalists must take while society works out other ways of solving the problems of moving illegal animal and plant products.

The peatlands: lessons not learned

Examples of the disastrous long-term effects of wetland conversion are easy to find, particularly in the North. But this has yet to prevent the mistakes from being repeated.

The English Fens provide an example. As early as the 19th Century, much attention was being paid to the problems of peat shrinkage in the Fens. A post, known as the Holme post, was sunk into the peat in 1848. It has since dramatically documented the sinking of the land — at an annual rate of about three centimetres — as the peat has compacted, oxidised and eroded. The post is now nearly four metres above the surrounding surface. Violent dust storms, particularly in 1929, emphasise how winds accelerate erosion and take their toll in crop losses and choked drains.

In many areas, the peat losses have exposed relatively infertile minerals, clays and sediments. These are much more expensive to farm and are less productive than either the original wetland ecosystem or much of the drained land, which includes a large proportion of Britain's 'grade one' farmland. That grading will need changing. Progressive sinking of the land surface has required larger and larger investments in drainage. One of the most recent grants for work in the Fens from the European Community was for £2 million ($2.8 million), of which half went to just one scheme at March, Cambridgeshire, where a more powerful pump was needed because of peat shrinkage.

Farming has cost the Fens — and will cost the farmers — more and more. While maintaining and improving drains becomes ever more expensive, long-term yields will doubtless fall, and farmers will try to counter this trend through the wasteful, expensive and environmentally damaging application of too much fertiliser. One 12th Century chronicler wrote of the area: "Here tis such quantity of fish as to cause astonishment in strangers" [132]. The fish have since disappeared. The waterfowl have declined to a tiny fraction of their original numbers, and only small vestiges of the original wetland remain.

Britain has no monopoly on peatland 'development' disasters. In Florida, the loss of peat soil has been estimated at 2.5 cm per year in parts of Florida. As early as 1929, the botanist John Small wrote a book entitled *From Eden to Sahara, Florida's Tragedy* documenting the hazards of draining the state's wetlands. New peat does not form on the drained land, and most of these soils are likely to be too shallow for agriculture by 1990-2000 [133].

The drained peat is particularly prone to fire; in the 1940s, large areas were burned to expose the underlying limestone. The rocky surface and lowered water table prevent any return to the original wetland habitat, even when the land is abandoned. Yet today even the exposed bedrock is being broken up by powerful machines. Crops like tomatoes and peppers grown under such 'hydroponic'-like conditions (using mixtures of water and fertiliser but no soil) require a great deal of both water and fertiliser.

The mistakes continue elsewhere. Papyrus peat has been drained and is disappearing fast in the Hula Valley of northern Israel near Lake

Kinneret (Galilee). Fires have burnt below the surface of the peat, suddenly opening up as chasms several metres in diameter. Frequent dust storms provide evidence of the unstable character and limited future of arable farming there. As more fertilisers are used on this land, there has been increased release of nitrogen and phosphorus into Lake Kinneret, the nation's most important water supply.

In Rwanda, peat drainage has turned the peat into dry particles, which do not 'turn back into' peat when water is added again. This process, which turned swamps into what one ecologist called a 'dusty desert' [134] was being referred to as the 'black death' as early as 1950 [135]. Despite all these experiences, drainage of the Marais Vernier in Normandy, France, proceeded, but because of the extent of peat shrinkage, the agricultural development of the area had to be abandoned.

In the tropics, organic matter is oxidised more quickly than in temperate zones, so drainage leads rapidly and inevitably to surface lowering. In East Africa and coastal peatlands, where sodium and not calcium is the dominant alkali metal and where sulphur levels are high, there is the added danger of large releases of acid sulphate.

Some of the drained peats of the Somerset Levels and the Norfolk Broads in Britain suffer this type of acidification. Apart from its direct impact on wetland organisms, this acidification can cause the release of toxic levels of iron, aluminium and manganese. Other studies have shown that heavy metals too can be released; increases in mercury and lead levels in one Scandinavian lake have been related to peat drainage [136]. More coliform bacteria are released from farmed land than from unreclaimed peat [137]. This may have been a significant factor in the contamination and recent closure of estuary oyster and clam fisheries in North Carolina [138].

In view of the importance of coastal and lake fisheries throughout the Third World, it makes sense to be clear about the possible consequences of agricultural development.

Chapter 8

Dams, barrages, canals and wetlands

The threats to wetlands posed by dams, barrages and canals are often countered by arguments for power generation, irrigation, improved communication and access to remote areas.

In many cases, industrialised countries have changed completely the natural regime of rivers to control water and meet the ever increasing demands of expanding cities and industries. The seasonally inundated floodplain marshes, swamps and forests of Europe and North America have contracted and been cut steadily into smaller and smaller segments. They remain significant landscape elements in only a few exceptional areas, such as the Mississippi Valley and parts of the Danube basin, and as constricted fringes of smaller rivers which have escaped development.

The bottomland hardwoods of the Mississippi basin and the riverine forests of Europe are becoming increasingly rare. The European loss became a national, then international, issue in 1984 and 1985 when opposition mounted to the Austrian government's plans to dam the Danube at Hainburg below Vienna, which would have destroyed one of the last great stretches of wet riverside forest in Europe, and a site listed under the Ramsar convention. In January 1985, the Austrian Supreme Court ruled in favour of the case presented by the World Wildlife Fund on behalf of several farmers who owned land in the forest, and Austrian Chancellor Fred Sinowatz subsequently agreed that alternative sites would be considered. But decisions like this are rare. More common is the steady loss of riverine forests and other important floodplain wetlands to virtually uncontrolled 'development'.

It would be nice to think that Ramsar membership was the real strength of argument in Austria, but the strength of feeling of thousands of protestors was of undoubted importance. Comparable levels of organised environmental awareness or information dissemination are as yet rare in developing countries, in spite of the fact that many rural Third World communities have a great affinity with their environment.

Dams like the Akosombo Dam in Ghana can — in theory — provide valuable hydroelectricity and irrigation water. But without careful planning they can disrupt fisheries, affect the wildlife dynamics of a floodplain, and displace pastoral and fishing communities.

Dams

Dams are a complex issue. On the one hand their reservoirs can displace large numbers of people; their irrigation waters can spread debilitating 'snail fever' (schistosomiasis/bilharzia) and other diseases across large areas; they can disrupt fisheries, land-use systems and natural ecosystems downstream; they can saddle poor governments with recurrent costs which cannot be met and demands in trained manpower which cannot be found. Many dams, especially in Africa, have not lived up to expectations; many officials at the World Bank and the Arab Bank for African Development admit privately they want nothing more to do with such schemes.

Yet dryland nations in Africa and throughout the Third World need to make more rational use of their water resources and grow more food. More than 150 dams are planned or have already been built in the Sahel, where the 1968-73 and 1984-85 droughts respectively alerted and emphasised to the developed world the problems of natural resource management in Africa. Africa needs more dams, but of the small-scale variety that can be realistically budgeted and managed. The planning of these dams cannot be left solely to the builders, but must include ecologists and agronomists, whose balance sheets reflect the problems as well as the promises of dams.

The popular view among politicians, aid officials and engineers is that major dams and their associated engineering schemes are vital for progress in the Third World. They bring electricity to parts of the world with few if any alternative energy sources; they can prevent flood disasters and improve communications; and they can irrigate the food crops of drought-stricken Africa and other dryland regions.

The first loan by the World Bank to a developing country — to Chile in 1948 — was for an irrigation and hydroelectric power project. By 1982, the Bank had loaned nearly $27 billion for agricultural programmes, with more than a third of the funds going to 285 irrigation schemes [139]. Despite the disillusionment among some development experts, the pace of dam-building is accelerating. By 1990 the world could have 113 dams higher than 150 metres — so-called 'superdams' — nearly half of which will have been built in the 1980s [140].

Dams, irrigation systems and their associated engineering structures all bring about far-reaching — and often drastic — changes in the ecology and management of floodplains and other wetlands. They reduce or eliminate downstream flooding cycles; alter water chemistry, discharge and sediment behaviour; and block or interrupt the migration of fish. They also create bodies of open water with their own new ecological systems, different from the previous river systems.

Dams have a major impact on fisheries and the other natural and economic assets of wetlands downstream. Nearly half the 1975 African freshwater fish catch of 1.4 million tonnes was thought to come from rivers; the proportion in Asia and Latin America is probably greater [141].

Garry Bernacsek, a consultant to the FAO Fisheries Resource Division, estimates that some 30% of the total African fish catch comes from inland fisheries [141a].

When dams stop seasonal flooding they reduce the capacity of downstream floodplains for feeding and breeding. The damage this can cause to fish stocks was seen on the Chari, Niger and Senegal rivers during the Sahelian drought of the early 1970s [142]. The decline in the fish catch on the Missouri River in the United States from 680 tonnes in 1894 to 122 tonnes in 1963 has been attributed largely to the loss of habitats that resulted from reservoir construction.

Studies of the effects of dam construction on the Colorado, the Volga and the Niger have all revealed significant changes in fish species composition, often with an increase in predatory species — a change which almost always means a fall in the total mass of fish in a body of water [143].

The reduction of the catch on the Colorado River — from 22,440 tonnes in 1911 to 6,800 in the 1970s — was attributed more to the disruption of fish migration and changes in flow than to the loss of floodplain [144]. In the Murray River, Australia, the 800-km migrations of the golden perch (*Plectroplites ambiguus*) have been prevented by flood control structures. On the Indus of Pakistan and in Brazilian Rivers, the migration patterns of many species have been seriously affected by dam closure [145]. The decline of the sardine fishery in the Eastern Mediterranean has even been attributed to the reduced silt and nutrient inputs caused by the building of the Aswan Dam on the Nile.

Dams create lakes which are often welcomed as new sources of protein, and indeed lakes can be extremely productive. But some scientists consider that this is often illusory; the great spurt in fish production which occurs during the first few years after flooding, when inundated vegetation and terrestrial nutrients and organisms are adding to available food supply, is rarely maintained without active fisheries management. Increased fish production occurred for five or six years in Lake Kariba (Zimbabwe/Zambia), before the system began to stabilise and catches fell off [146].

The improved fisheries argument was used to support the displacement of 35,000 inhabitants by the creation in 1982 of the Lagdo reservoir on the Bénoué in Cameroon. The downstream fishery has been cut by half, but consultants believe the potential of the lake is almost twice that of the original river [147]. But catches from reservoirs are usually about the same — or at best slightly higher — as catches from floodplains. One reason for this may be that not enough attention has been paid to how the potential of reservoirs can be maximised through careful management.

The final equation must include not just the fishery potential of the new lake, but also the value of all the other wetland resources that are lost. Eugene Balon of the University of Guelph, Canada, holds that the total potential food production of Lake Kariba can never better the potential of the undisturbed Gwembe Valley before the Kariba Dam was built: "Wild animals alone, if harvested, could have yielded the same amount of protein as the lake ... In addition there was space along the river for intensive agricultural use, and a much higher potential harvest is possible at a lower energy cost in the river alluvium than on the escarpment or plateau." This view is supported by observations of fish losses below the Kainji on the Niger in Nigeria and below the Pa Mong in the Mekong [148].

If plans proceed to build 11 new dams on tributaries of the Niger in Mali, Guinea, Ivory Coast and Burkina Faso (formerly Upper Volta) and two on the Baui River close to the inner delta, the future of the 100,000 semi-nomadic Bozo and Somono fishermen, catching 90% of Mali's fish production worth 3% of the GNP, looks at best uncertain.

Wetland habitat, wildlife and man

Loss of floodplain not only reduces the area of swamps and temporarily inundated land, but the reduced flow of water can produce stretches of stagnant water and residual pools that harbour disease-carrying organisms, such as mosquitoes, and promote the invasion of alien plant species. The spread of the water hyacinth throughout much of Africa, Asia, Australia and the southern United States has been helped by artificial canals and abandoned river channels; the water hyacinth often overwhelms native plant species, such as the Nile cabbage (*Pistia stratiotes*) in Africa.

Dams can affect the wildlife dynamics of a floodplain. Some species, like the Kafue lechwe (a small antelope) of Zambia, have a reproductive and migratory pattern closely linked to the flooding cycle. Since the building of the Kafue Gorge Dam in 1972, wet season discharge has been cut to maintain a steady flow in the dry season for power generation. Generally drier conditions and reduced nutrient inputs from sediment mean that the floodplain now produces less vegetation, and the lechwe and other wild herbivores must compete more with cattle for what there is. Before the dam there was a stable population of about 94,000 lechwe, but the population has fallen to about 50,000 [148]. There are real fears that without careful management, numbers will keep on falling.

In South America the capybara (*Hydrochoerus hydrochaeris* — a large rodent) is an abundant floodplain resident. The loss of its floodplain habitat poses little if any danger of extinction for the capybara itself, but by restricting the species more to the permanent swamps, more pressure will be exerted on the often rarer and more vulnerable species of the swamps. Threatened species may find their once stable niches collapsing in the competition for limited resources and living space.

Many of the African and South American floodplains threatened by dam schemes are exceptionally important breeding, feeding and wintering grounds for waterfowl and other birds. One example is the inner delta of the Niger, the winter home of enormous populations of water birds. The floodplains of the Amazon basin and rivers further south are key resting points or winter habitat for migratory species from the North American Arctic.

People too will be affected. Lifestyles and cultures have revolved around wetland cycles in Africa for hundreds and perhaps thousands of

118

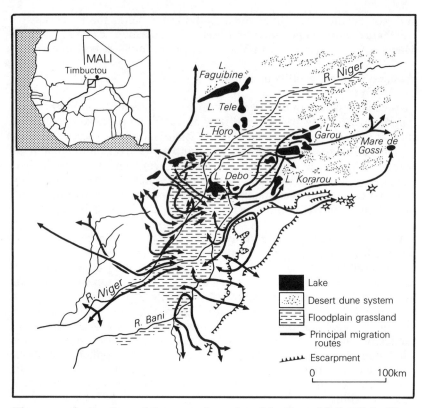

The seasonal migrations of the pastoral peoples of the Central Delta of the Niger.
Source: after Gallais 1967, in Welcomme 1979.

years. The seasonal migrations of people like the Nuer and Dinka of the Sudan's vast Sudd swamp; of pastoral tribes such as the Tuareg, Warbé, Sonhabé and Peuhl of the inner delta of the Niger, and the Ba Tswana of the Okavango in Botswana are key examples of situations repeated throughout the continent's wetlands.

Some scientists feel that the large numbers of cattle grazing in and around the wetlands play an important role in maintaining productivity and especially fish production in the floodplain. Changes in ecosystems caused by dams require new ways of life, such as resettlement or permanent settlement for the first time, and adjustment to an alien economy based on sedentary agriculture, irrigation, controlled grazing and the cash-dominated market place.

Barrages

Barrages are similar to dams, but tend to be built to control flows in estuaries or coastal bays. The barrage across the Zuider Zee in the Netherlands, for example, created Lake Ijssel and caused a major change in fisheries ecology.

Various barrage proposals have been made which would affect important coastal wetlands in Britain. Shelved several times for economic reasons, the scheme to put a hydroelectric barrage across the Severn in western England is still very much alive. Possible impacts include:

* loss of inter-tidal mudflats and salinity changes, which will reduce the habitat and feeding area of waterfowl in the Severn estuary — one of the most important international sites in Europe;
* possible disruption of commercially important migratory fish — particularly salmon and eels worth £6.4 million a year;
* a decline in oxygen and increased eutrophication in upstream waters;
* increased pressure on wetland and other habitats due to development and other recreational activities.

Britain's Nature Conservancy Council is expected to object to the £6 billion scheme, if or when it receives a government go-ahead. As yet no full environmental impact study has been made of the plan.

Polders

A 'polder' is an area of low land surrounded by dykes. The dykes keep normal water rises from reaching this area of floodplain or coast, and allow more controlled and intensive agriculture within the impounded area, independent of natural flood regimes. This invariably reduces habitat diversity.

About a quarter of the land area of the Netherlands is below mean sea level; most of this is impoldered and protected against flooding by a complex system of dykes and dams built over a period of centuries. There are now major plans to develop polders in some of the floodplains of Africa. They would need massive capital investment and sophisticated drainage and irrigation control. To justify their construction, planners would need to put high return agricultural enterprises on the 'reclaimed' land. This would often mean cash rather than food crops, and a few large mechanised plantations rather than many small farms. This would bring further change to the floodplains by encouraging the building of roads, railways, housing and towns.

		Area (ha)
Tana Delta	Kenya	16,000
Angaw Basin Project	Ghana	25,000
Sebon River Basin	Morocco	43,000
Niger Delta	Nigeria	17,650
Hadejia Valley	Nigeria	20,000
Nyawarongo Project	Rwanda	10,000
Kafue Flats	Zambia	70,000
Benone Valley	Cameroon	29,000

Proposed polder projects in Africa.

Plans to impolder 16,000 hectares of the Tana delta in Kenya, largely to grow rice, will reduce the dry season stock grazing areas of the Orma tribe and increase the pressure from both livestock and extensive wild animal populations on the remaining floodplain. Fish yields may fall by 700 tonnes per year, and the loss of nearly half the riverine and floodplain forest will pose a major threat to the rich monkey fauna.

No one can predict how the altered flow patterns will change the form of the river. The water will be polluted by the pesticides and herbicides recommended in the feasibility study by a group of consulting engineers. Development costs are 15 times higher than those of upland rice schemes. Consultants conclude that alternatives are needed, both for Kenyan rice production and for the development of the delta.

Canals and the wetlands of Louisiana

River 'canalisation' usually involves straightening, smoothing and deepening channels, and/or raising natural levees (raised ground along riverbanks). The usual aim is to reduce flooding and improve navigation, but the process can remove or cut water off from natural fringing wetland habitats. It also alters natural river features such as pools, which have important functions in fish migration and other wildlife patterns.

Canals have also been built independent of natural channels. A remarkably dense network of canals now occupies 2-4% of the wetland area of coastal Louisiana. Built for oil and gas recovery, navigation and other purposes, they are only part of the long process of levee building and heightening since the European settlement of New Orleans. Some canals in the Mississippi delta were dug by fur-trappers in the early period of settlement, so they could manoeuvre their small boats through the marsh. Regular use and erosion has made them much bigger and more visible. US wetland researcher W.D. Davies contends that they affect drainage patterns and salinity, and stand as "a reminder of man's abilities to unknowingly change the delicate balance in the natural system" [150]. Much larger canals have been excavated, first to exploit the swamp forests (particularly the cypress), and then to penetrate the difficult wetland terrain in the search for and development of huge oil and gas reserves.

An estimated 10% of the wetlands in Barataria Bay in the Mississippi delta have been lost as a direct result of canal construction [151]. But canal widening is increasing annually at 2-14% [152]. Eugene Turner and John Day of the Center for Wetland Resources, Louisiana State University, warn that canals may eventually be the main cause of land loss in Louisiana. Land losses from human activities in the coastal zone already run to more than four sq km per year, producing staggering direct and indirect costs. Canals destroy habitat, both directly (through dredging and the disposal of dredged material) and indirectly (by changing water flow patterns). The canals bring in salt water, a process encouraged by natural sinking in the delta region and the loss of marsh functions such as water purification and storm buffering.

Canal construction has caused annual losses to fisheries worth $2.1-4.3 million (equivalent to $3.6-7.1 million at present values). Add to this the indirect economic values of fishing, such as boat building, and the cumulative economic loss comes to at least $8.5 million per year, and possibly as much as $17 million [153]. Eugene Turner estimates that 1% of wetlands will be lost each year over the next 20 years, costing the commercial fishing industry a total of $1.08 billion. If the land loss could be reduced by only 10%, he suggests, the annual savings would be $5 million [154].

The Jonglei

For more than 50 years there have been plans to divert the Nile from the swamps of the southern Sudan — the Sudd (meaning 'barrier' in Arabic) — to save water lost to evaporation and to improve communications between northern and southern Sudan. The Sudd is often described as the world's largest swamp; within the Jonglei region of southern Sudan it consists of 11,000 sq km of seasonally inundated floodplain — an area the size of Jamaica. It is sustained by flows from the White Nile and its tributaries.

As with so many of the world's wetlands, remoteness and inaccessability has so far protected from 'development' the complex Jonglei ecosystem of permanent swamp with papyrus, Nile cabbage,

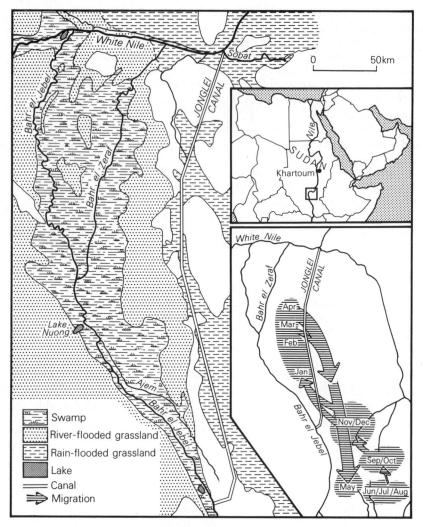

The seasonal migrations of the pastoral peoples of the Jonglei region.

other aquatic plants and periodically flooded grasslands. It has flourished as a prime habitat for birds and large herbivores, and is a particularly important link in the chain of sites along the Nile Valley for species migrating between the tropics and Eurasia. The people of the Sudd and its surrounding areas — the Dinka, Nuer and Shilluk tribes (200-400,000 people in all) — have developed life patterns involving pastoral migration, agriculture and fishing, all closely geared to the cycle of seasonal flooding and ecological diversity of the Sudd.

In 1978, construction began on the Jonglei Canal, at 350 km twice as long as Suez. It was meant to provide an additional 4.75 billion cubic metres of water a year for irrigation and urban/industrial use, to be shared equally between Egypt and the Sudan. The canal was initially scheduled for completion in 1983, but because of technical and engineering difficulties, funding problems and armed conflict in the area, it is unlikely to be finished until at least the end of the decade. By the end of 1984, 260 km had been excavated along a route from Bor to Malakal.

The canal will reduce the water flow into the swamp by up to 20 million cubic metres per day. It will also have far-reaching implications for both wildlife and people previously adjusted to the wetland flooding cycles. Controversy rages over the expected impacts. A report by a study team from the Anglo-Italian consultancy firm Mefit-Babtic, supported by European Community funds, predicts reductions of 21-80% for the swamp and 17-58% for the floodplain depending on actual — and in the long term unpredictable — river discharges from the Equatorial lakes.

The Mefit-Babtic team told the Royal Geographical Society of Britain in 1982 that, overall, the canal would help the local population. But after further analysis of the data, they retracted that statement. Their final draft report says that not only will the swamps and floodplain contract, but the quality of grazing lands will deteriorate more than expected [155]. "The facts oblige us to hold a less optimistic view now", the draft concludes [156].

The Jonglei supports populations of the endangered shoebill stork (*Balaeniceps rex*), and possibly the largest number of water birds anywhere in Africa. There are nearly half a million tiang antelope (*Damaliscus lunatus tiang*), constituting one of the world's largest remaining populations of wild large mammals. Most of the wild populations of the Nile lechwe are also found in the Jonglei, as are buffalo, elephant, gazelle, hippopotami, white eared kob, reedbuck, waterbuck and zebra. Stephen Cobb, Mefit-Babtic study team's director for range ecology, has warned that "a reduction in the area of the floodplain will threaten all of these...." [157] Cobb feels that the canal itself threatens the large animal migrants. He cites evidence from

Anne Charnock/Earthscan

The Sudd swamp of southern Sudan supports as many as 400,000 tribal pastoralists, farmers and fishermen, whose lives are closely geared to its seasonal flooding and ecological diversity. But the construction of the 350-km Jonglei Canal threatens to reduce the flow of water into the Sudd, with far-reaching implications for people and wildlife.

studies of wildebeest in the Serengeti (Tanzania) to support the view that many animals will drown in attempting canal crossings. Some 90% of the Jonglei tiang are migratory and will need to cross the canal twice a year, including one crossing — in March/April — with small calves. He notes that the canal and the road alongside will allow increased hunting. Hence stable wildlife populations, in equilibrium with present harvesting, may in future dwindle to critical levels and even disappear. The problems posed by the canal itself could be overcome or deferred if crossing points for both wildlife and domestic livestock were set up, and reserves created where hunting and poaching could be restricted [158].

It is one thing to legislate controls against the traditional activities of often fiercely independent people though, and quite another to enforce them. Up to 25% of the meat in their diet comes from hunting wild herbivores, particularly reedbuck and mongella gazelle. Commercial and subsistence fishing provides an estimated 30,000 tonnes per year.

The Nuer and Dinka herders are expert at exploiting the floodplain cycle. As the dry season progresses, the cattle follow the receding floodwaters towards the permanent swamp and graze the fertile 'toich' (a Dinka word meaning temporary swamps), where grass production may be 2-3 times that of areas receiving only rainwater. During the dry season there can be more than 750,000 cattle on the floodplain. At the beginning of the flood, around May, people and cattle begin to return from the toich pastures to permanent settlements on the uplands, where they practice some subsistence cultivation. During the wet season their cattle can severely overgraze these areas [159]. The Shilluk tribes are more sedentary, and their villages on elevated ground alongside the White Nile are very close to the toich, thereby reducing the need for movement. But the canal is bound to restrict the movements of people and their herds.

There are conflicting views about the future of the fisheries. They may increase with the permanent canal and improved access to fishing grounds, or they may decline due to the drying up of lakes and to overfishing. The Zeraf Nuer tribe stand to lose the most; they changed from pastoralism to fishing after 1961, when higher discharge levels from the upstream lakes caused flooding of much of Zeraf Island. A partial reduction in water level could dramatically reduce fishing.

People and cattle will be drawn to the canal both to use the water and because the canal will become a centre for communications and commerce. It may also become a centre for water-related disease, especially schistosomiasis, which has already spread throughout the Sudan's irrigation network and been passed on to labourers from far away who work seasonally on the irrigated farmland. Under the normal floodplain regime, the dry season kills the snails which carry the disease.

Improved communications associated with the canal and easier access to market economies in the north may in turn encourage sales of the best animals and reductions in herd quality. The canal will also tempt young people into the towns and cities. All of this — putting pastoralists more firmly into the money economy and offering the youth of a region broader opportunities — may be seen as part of the 'development' process. But unless the possible losses of cattle and human resources can be replaced by other reliable sources of livelihood, the region could become a vast poverty belt. Development writer Anne Charnock has warned that the Jonglei region could easily become dependent on food aid.

A.E. El Moghraby and M.O. El Sammani (respectively team leader of the government's Swamp Ecology Group and former team leader of the Socio-economic Unit of the Jonglei Executive Organ) have urged critics of the scheme to take full account of its benefits: prevention of flooding, increase of land for agriculture, year-round water, new fisheries, greater employment, reduction in swamp disease vectors, improved communications between Juba and the capital, stimulation of the agricultural and industrial economy, and trade in a neglected area. "The new mode [of life] will be a more satisfactory one than that which exists at present", they contend.

This touches the underlying dilemma facing all wetlands development. There is no doubt that development can bring advantages, but all too often the disadvantages are not appreciated. The social or economic benefits can only be sustained by environmental support. If environmental alteration of the floodplain causes irreversible losses of habitat and species, or prevents the use of resources, then the 'new mode of life' may cost dearly.

The lessons of Kissimmee

Realisation of the problems which can result from running canals through wetlands has led to a remarkable policy change in Florida — an expensive turnabout which could in the long term save governments with similar canal-building plans a great deal of money.

In the 1960s, the US Army Corps of Engineers built a $29 million canal along Florida's Kissimmee River to control seasonal floods which washed over the riverbanks and damaged property and farmland. Flooding had been particularly severe in 1947 and 1948.

But the canal had a disastrous effect. Some 8,000 hectares of marshland were lost, resulting in a major decline in wildlife. The number of bald eagles fell by nearly 75%, and of some waterfowl species by more than 90% [160]. Before the canal, the naturally sinuous course of the Kissimmee slowed floods resulting from storms. The marginal wetlands not only helped control floods, but acted as chemical filters on the water passing through them. After the canal was built, farmers moved quickly onto the new protected floodplain. More water was running off the area because there was no wetland vegetation to slow it; this runoff carried large amounts of fertiliser from the farmland, and oxygen supplies in Lake Okeechobee were quickly depleted.

A 1972 University of Miami report concluded that "the canal was a major factor in accelerated lake eutrophication, with resultant water quality deterioration". It recommended halting the discharge of all waste materials into the basin and developing a plan for reflooding the marshes of the Lower Kissimmee Valley [161]. In 1976 the State Legislature passed the Kissimmee River Restoration Act, and the South Florida Water Management District is now preparing to spend more than twice as much as it cost to build the canal to return the river to its original course.

Work has started on a demonstration project that over the next 15 years is meant to develop into full restoration of the marginal wetlands. "Our goal," says state governor Bob Graham, "is that by the year 2000, the water system will look and function more as it did in the year 1900 than it does today" [162]. Despite the delays in its implementation, the decision points the way to wider acceptance of the vital role of natural wetlands in the economic and ecologically sound management of water resources.

Channelling and damming the future

China has plans to divert water from the Chang Jaing (Yangtse) River to irrigate nearly four million hectares in the arid north. Major canals are being built in India to take water from the Brahmaputra, Ganges and Indus Rivers to drought-affected areas in Madhya Pradesh, Rajasthan and Tamil Nadu. Even more ambitious are the proposals of the North American Nawapa project, which would channel water from Alaska and Canada to irrigate areas thousands of kilometres away in the southwest United States and Mexico [163].

In the Philippines, an estimated 861 dams are planned [164]. In the Amazon basin, 40 dams have been proposed, affecting every major river. Three large dams have recently been completed: the Curna-una Dam near Santareus in Para (10,000 hectare reservoir), the Paredao Dam on the Araguari River in Amapa (10,000 hectares) and the Tucurui Dam on the Tocantius River in Para (246,000 hectares). Initial studies of the Curna-una Dam have indicated adverse affects on fish, mass development of aquatic plants and deterioration in water quality [165].

Despite the evidence of serious ecological and environmental consequences, major water engineering schemes are still proposed which would devastate some of South America's finest wetlands. Construction of dams and canals for irrigation and power production threatens the once remote Pantanal do Mato Grosso, arguably South America's most important wetland. Covering an area of over 100,000 sq km — larger than Hungary — it is a region of seasonally flooded savannas, with scattered palms, many small freshwater lakes and marshland.

Plans in the Soviet Union to block the River Ob and pump water through Kazakhstan to irrigate land 1,500 km away in the drier south are well advanced. The drainage waters from these irrigation projects may make up for some of the water now being taken from the Aral Sea for industry and irrigation. But salts leached from the soil will undoubtedly reduce the quality of this water. The impacts of reduced flow on the Arctic floodplains of the Ob and coastal waters of Siberia are a cause of great concern to scientists, both inside and outside the Soviet Union. But as nothing quite like this vast experiment has ever been tried before, it is hard to predict what will actually happen.

One of the main problems in assessing the impacts on wetlands of major schemes — and arguing against their continuation — is the absence of 'base-line' data: information on conditions before and after change.

Edward Goldsmith and Nicholas Hildyard, in their 1985 study of big dams worldwide [166], argue vociferously against the 'superdam' approach on the grounds that such schemes bring far-reaching environmental and ecological problems, cause social misery through resettlement and cultural impacts, increase the incidence of disease, and widen the gap between the beneficiaries of the schemes ("...large multinational companies, the urban elites of the Third World and the politicians who commissioned the projects...") and the people on whose behalf the projects are allegedly undertaken.

Chapter 9

Peatlands — a burning issue

Peat has been used as a fuel in the Northern hemisphere for at least 2,000 years. Laboriously-cut sods, dried outdoors by sun and wind, are still the main energy source for domestic heating and cooking for many remote communities in Northwest and Central Europe, where other energy sources may be expensive or scarce.

There are virtually no houses on the western highlands and islands of Scotland that do not rely on peat. In Ireland it has been a traditional fuel for centuries. Since the turn of the century there has been a growth in the use of peat on an industrial scale for boilers and large-scale power and district heating plants. Fuel peat production worldwide nearly doubled between 1950 and 1980, from 47 million tonnes to about 90 million tonnes [167]. In the USSR, easily the largest producer, 47 state electric generating stations and 32 combined heat and power plants use milled peat. Yet overall, peat contributes less than 1.5% of total Soviet energy consumption (though the proportion is significantly higher in Western Russia) [168].

Finland too is aggressively developing its peat resources, with 90% of that cut being used to generate power. Some 3.1 million tonnes were produced in 1980, but 8-10 million tonnes per year is the target for 1990 [169]. Peat provides about 2% of the nation's energy requirements. Peat mining, along with draining for farming and afforestation, will completely destroy the majority of mid-Finland's raised bogs before the end of the century, if the present rate of exploitation continues. Canada and Sweden are looking into ways of using peat for energy on a large scale.

As late as 1969, the world was thought to have 150 million hectares of peatlands, mostly in the North. But the estimate today is 500 million hectares [170], and more and more deposits are being found throughout the tropical Third World.

Ireland: State support and private enterprise

Since 1946, the Irish Peat Development Authority (Bord na Mona) has mined more than 8,000 hectares of bog for a range of fuel and horticultural products. The authority's glossy promotional literature

Country	Fuel peat	Horticultural peat	Total
USSR	32,000	48,600	80,600
Ireland	2,255	153	2,408
Finland	1,255	202	1,457
West Germany	101	810	911
China	323	526	849
United States	0	324	324
Canada	0	198	198
Poland	0	113	113
Sweden	0	109	109
Czechoslovakia	0	109	109
East Germany	0	69	69
Britain	no data	69	69
France	20	40	60
Denmark	0	44	44
Norway	0.4	33	33.4
New Zealand	0	4	4
Others	41	1,174	1,215
TOTAL	c 36,000	c 52,000	c 88,000

World fuel peat and horticultural peat production 1980 (in '000 tonnes per hectare). Source: Bord na Mona 1984.

says that this has "created wealth out of what had been wasteland" [171]. Over 40% of the country's electricity is generated from seven peat-fuel power stations. The authority employs 7,000 people, mainly in remote rural areas where other jobs are scarce. Peat makes major savings for the nation's balance of payments. This is especially true of the *Sphagnum* moss peat which forms the relatively undecomposed fibrous upper layers of many bogs and is much favoured for horticulture. Ireland exports more than a million cubic metres of horticultural peat worldwide, exports worth $18 million (IR£16 million) in 1983-84.

Bord na Mona now offers government grants encouraging private enterprise to exploit bogs not suitable for large-scale development by the Authority. It sees this as a way of turning "an even greater proportion of Ireland's peat resources ... into wealth". Private enterprise already produces up to a million tonnes of sod peat annually. Development has been further encouraged by peat consultancy firms, such as the Herbst Group, which markets equipment and systems

Land use	Preparation	Cost (IR£/ha)
Grassland	Surface cultivation	600
Grassland	Deep ploughing	1,000
Cereals	Surface cultivation	750
Vegetables	Surface cultivation	750
Forestry	Direct planting	700
Biomass-Energy	Surface cultivation	2,500

Reclamation costs for mined out peatland in Ireland, January 1984.

allowing the "smallest bogs [to] be economically exploited, ... the highest tonnage removed annually" [172].

A 'chain-saw' sod extractor marketed by Herbst leaves the ground surface intact while extracting the underlying peat as a long core. Herbst promotes this by claiming that it creates minimum environmental damage. But while the surface remains relatively intact, the operation destroys the 'human services' of peat bogs — water and nutrient controls, scientific values and geochemical storage.

There is considerable appeal in the longer term utilisation of cut-over (mined out) peatlands as agricultural or forestry land. Proximity to mineral soil and improved drainage conditions creates conditions where reclamation can be economically appealing. This is illustrated in recent costs from Ireland (see figure).

The attractions of peat energy

Several factors have encouraged peat-rich nations, particularly those poor in other sources of energy, to consider developing their wetlands for energy.

Petroleum shortages in the 1970s alerted governments to the need to diversify into other energy sources. The pressure comes not only from oil. The coal miners' strike in Britain in 1984-85 stimulated an increase in peat extraction from Scottish bogs and resulted in considerable sales of specialised equipment from Ireland. Companies too are looking for ways to reduce energy costs. The Georgia-Pacific Corporation in the United States, mainly a paper company, has bought over 2,000 hectares in the Santa Fe wetland of north central Florida with the intention of mining peat as fuel for a pulpwood factory.

US ecologist Marjorie Winkler, of the University of Wisconsin, estimates that peatland mining in the United States could supply less than 20 years of national public energy requirements (heat and electricity), but peat may be more appealing to individual states. Development of 405,000 hectares of peatland in Minnesota (about 12% of the state's total) to a depth of about three metres would provide the state with enough energy for 32 years [173].

The US Department of Energy has funded state peatland inventories, and consultancy firms have done their own surveys. The US Synthetic Fuels Corporation (SFC) has funded peat conversion projects in North Carolina and Maine. Construction began in 1982 in North Carolina of a $250 million methanol plant planned to produce 194 million litres per year. The original, much higher, funding plans fell through, but the scheme may well be resurrected with private financial support. Other organisations are actively considering peat energy programmes in the pocosins [174].

Marjorie Winkler and Calvin DeWitt (of the University of Michigan) suggest that the enormous grant from SFC for the peat methanol project in North Carolina could be better used directly in the coastal communities. They are concerned that neither this effort nor the attempts to harvest peat in Maine for energy have been evaluated for environmental and ecological impacts [174a].

Several new technologies have been developed, which have encouraged peat usage. The 'slurry pond' method allows mechanical extractors to be floated on barges in open water within the peat, which is cut and then pumped to dewatering sites. New methods of mechanically removing the water from peat enables the mining of waterlogged, submerged peat or of deposits located close to sea level, where solar drying may be impracticable. This is of interest to tropical and sub-tropical countries where drainage of coastal, riverside and lakeside wetlands is uneconomic and impracticable, and solar drying impeded either by humidity or lack of space. Wet bogs once thought uneconomic for energy use may now become attractive investments.

There are also now better and more efficient ways of burning peat. 'Gasification' involves heating peat to produce a gas which is then burned; 'fluidised bed combustion' involves passing an air stream through a bed of solid particles which behave like a boiling liquid, making combustion cleaner and more complete. Research in Scandinavia and the United States is aiming to reduce the costs of turning peat into more flexible fuels, such as methanol. The goal is to make this form of energy cheaper than natural gas.

Tropical peat

Peat is not usually associated with tropical or sub-tropical environments, so Third World countries have been surprised by just how much peat has been turned up by recent inventories.

Peat production for energy began in Burundi in 1977 with the establishment of the Office national de la tourbe (ONATOUR — National Peat Office), working under the Ministry of Public Works, Energy and Mines to survey, extract, commercialise and popularise the use of peat. Only 50 tonnes were dug (by hand) in that first year, but 4,000 tonnes were harvested in 1980, and this was expected to increase to 30,000 tonnes in 1985. Sod production at Busoro, Rwanda, started in 1980, but hard cutting of peat was already established at Kiguhu Bog in the northern part of the country before 1978 to dry pyrethrum flowers for the insecticide industry. Marketing problems have left it with an uncertain future.

China has long used peat as a fuel, but it produces only 800,000 tonnes per year. Its reserves (estimated at 27 billion tonnes) have yet to be fully exploited. Indonesia is becoming interested in using its vast peat reserves, including the undisturbed deposits in the forests of Kalimantan and Irian Jaya.

'Peat aid'. The drive to harvest peat for fuel is supported by foreign aid and bilateral and multilateral agencies. Almost all the studies of peat energy potential in the Third World have been carried out by Northern consultants, agencies or companies. The potential of 'indigenous energy resources' has become fashionable among major funding agencies. Thus the industry department of the World Bank engaged Bord na Mona to prepare a report on fuel peat in developing countries, to help the Bank develop fuel peat as a local energy source.

Fears that woodfuel supplies will run out give added urgency to the new interest in tropical peat energy. In many developing nations, as much as 90% of domestic energy is supplied by wood. Population growth, particularly in urban areas, is leading to increased demand for wood for cooking and heating, which is in turn contributing to the loss of forest cover; the UN Food and Agriculture Organization (FAO) estimates that 11.3 million hectares of forest are lost annually, with 75% of that in the tropics and most of the rest from the semi-arid belt. By the year 2000, some 2.4 billion rural people will be using fuelwood faster than it is replenished [175].

'Peat aid' is appealing to aid agencies and politicians for two main reasons:

* both tend to see the exploitation of peat bogs as making energy out of 'worthless' land;
* the provision by peat-exploiting nations of help to less developed nations to do the same provides a shop window for technical expertise, an opportunity for large-scale engineering trials and a potential vehicle for the promotion of other goods and services.

In some cases, consultancy teams and funding agencies are falling over themselves. The first detailed inventory of peat deposits in Burundi was carried out in 1974 by Ruston Technical Services International for the UN Industrial Development Organization. In 1978, the US Agency for International Development (USAID) provided $490,000 to help Burundi's National Peat Office develop peat reserves for non-industrial use, and in 1980 a further $80 million was allocated over a five-year period. In 1979 and 1984, Bord na Mona carried out studies of valley bogs. A study by a Finnish company of the extensive peat system along the Akanyaru River was financed by the UN Development Programme (UNDP). Meanwhile, the Finnish government and Finnish industry, the World Bank, UNDP, and the Burundian Government are all looking into the possibilities of using the Akanyaru peat in connection with a nickel project at Musongati.

Yet all this investment has so far failed in its main stated aim: to reduce the national rate of deforestation in Burundi, one of the highest in Africa. In 1982, domestic and craft industry customers bought only 2% of ONATOUR's total sales of peat [176]. Eventual success may rest on the development of a suitable peat-burning stove, but it has as yet proved impossible to change traditional cooking and heating practices. And while attempts to overcome market resistance continue, *both* the forests and the wetlands are lost.

In Jamaica, the Finnish government and Finnish industry have been involved in engineering feasibility studies, investigating the wet mining of peat, mechanical dewatering, and combustion to generate electricity, using the Negril and Black River Lower Morass. Studies of Senegal's peat resources are being financed by UN agencies, France, West Germany, Canada, Finland and the European Development Fund. An assessment of fuel peat production in Indonesia is being funded by the Dutch Government. In Brazil, where many peatlands are still untouched, investigations on behalf of the Ministry of Mines and Energy are being carried out in consultation with Canadian industry.

Bord na Mona emphasised in their 1984 report to the World Bank that "the hydrological and other environmental effects resulting from peatland exploitation should be carefully examined prior to the commencement of development operations, in order to avoid irreversible damage". But in almost all Third World schemes, only small proportions of the budget, if any, are devoted to environmental assessments of project impacts and amelioration. Recent exceptions have been the environmental feasibility studies carried out in Jamaica by Swedish scientists supported by the Swedish Commission for Technical Cooperation.

The impact of peat mining

It is impossible to mine peat on a large scale without destroying habitat and ecosystems. Mining uses up peat many times faster than it is renewed. Concern over the rates at which peat and peatlands were vanishing led the International Union for Conservation of Nature and Natural Resources (IUCN) and the International Biological Programme to establish Operation Telma in the early 1970s, which drew up a list of peatlands of international importance and began to promote their conservation. The IUCN 14th General Assembly in 1978 urged governments "to take urgent measures to conserve an adequate and representative series of peatlands in their countries for the use of future generations, in biological and water resource management, scientific research and for amenity purposes" [177].

Development in the pocosin peatlands of North Carolina has left only 31% of the freshwater evergreen shrub bogs undisturbed, and the threats from mining continue to grow. Not only will an extensive and inaccessible wildlife reservoir become fragmented and largely disappear, but endangered plants such as the Venus fly trap, arrowleaf shieldwort (*Peltandra sagittaefolia*), spring flowering golden rod (*Solidago verna*) and rough leaf lustrife (*Lysimachia asperulaefolia*) will become extinct in the wild [178].

The key role played by peatlands in the hydrological and biochemical cycles — especially in the carbon cycle — are in danger of collapsing. As well as acting as a carbon sink in the past (see Chapter 4), peatlands currently store heavy metals, atmospheric fallout of minerals and particles, and nutrients fixed by plants before they die and add to the peat.

Jamaica: A case study. In 1979, the Jamaican government established the Petroleum Corporation of Jamaica (PCJ), and included in its mandate the exploitation of peat resources for electricity generation. The government was keen on the possibility of saving over $20 million a year in foreign exchange. Using 'wet excavation' techniques, the possibility has been explored of peat extraction from the coastal peatlands of the Negril and Black River Lower Morasses, which make up more than 75% of all Jamaica's wetlands, and represent wildlife habitats important not only for the Caribbean but for the entire Neotropics.

In 1981 a preliminary survey was carried out by the Natural Resources Conservation Department (NRCD) and the US-based consultants Traverse Group Inc. (TGI), following original engineering proposals made by engineering consultants from Ireland. The NRCD/TGI report was highly critical of the environmental and socio-economic consequences of the initial scheme, which included moving excavated peat by barge. There was particular concern about:

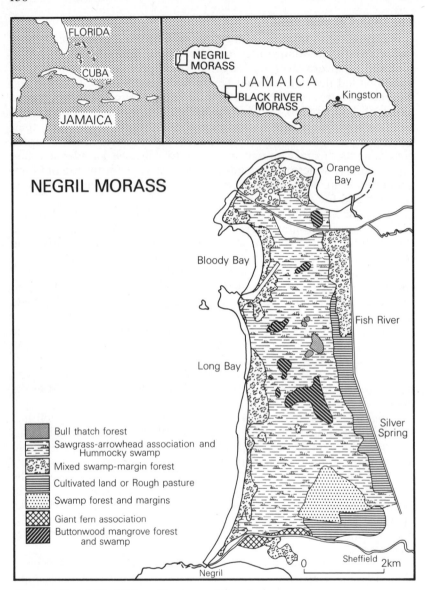

The Negril and Black River Morasses of Jamaica.

* the replacement of wetland by lake systems;
* the loss of habitat for shrimp, a key element in the food chain of commercially important fish, and an important harvest in its own right;
* the loss of habitat (particularly at Black River) for endangered and rare species, including crocodiles, manatees, aquatic birds and species of plants endemic to the area;
* reductions in the nursery and feeding areas of important species of fish (snapper, jack, snook, tarpon, mullet, anchovies and herring) and shrimp;
* social disruption to the local inhabitants.

A particular problem in the Negril Morass, especially since major drainage efforts in 1959, is the illicit cultivation of marijuana or 'ganja' (*Cannabis sativa*), which has brought burning, clearing and localised drainage to the marsh and parts of the highly valued swamp palm forest. The original NRCD/TGI report suggested that "from the political, legal or moral perspectives", the ending of the ganja industry may well be seen as a benefit of mining. But, the report went on, "it is unlikely ... that foreign exchange savings on ... the national energy account can offset the foregone earnings of the Negril ganja economy. Illegality aside for the moment, it is the earnings of ganja which underpin Negril's prosperity directly as well as indirectly through the tourist economy. In the past it has been admitted that these earnings have lubricated the wheels of urban industry as well."

The NRCD/TGI report recommended that an evaluation of the engineering, economic and environmental aspects of energy and non-energy alternatives (such as further capitalising on the tourist industry) be made prior to a decision being taken on peat mining. A new programme of engineering and environmental feasibility studies was commissioned, financed with grants of nearly US$1 million from the Swedish and Finnish governments. There were two phases to the investigations.

Phase 1: An environmental feasibility study (Feb 1982-Sept 1983). Undertaken by a Swedish team headed by Professor Sven Bjork, Institute of Limnology, University of Lund, and a PCJ team headed by Dr Barry Wade, Director of Environmental and Special Projects, its objectives were:

(i) to develop a better understanding of the present status of the Negril and Black River wetlands and how they function;
(ii) to develop criteria for the peat extraction process so as to cause the least possible environmental impact on the wetlands; and hence
(iii) to devise a satisfactory method of peat extraction; and

Edward Maltby

The sawgrass expanses of the Negril Morass in Jamaica. Plans to mine peat in the Morass for fuel have become an emotive political issue. The Petroleum Corporation of Jamaica has established experimental ponds (below) to examine the possible effects of the peat mining.

Edward Maltby

(iv) to advise on a programme of wetland management during and after peat extraction.

To achieve these objectives, researchers studied the ecological history of the wetlands, recorded existing ecological conditions, and made ecological forecasts using experimental excavated lakes. The results have been documented in a report by Bjork [179].

Phase 2: A wetland resource utilisation study. This set out to evaluate potential wetland resources, and outline detailed plans on how these resources could best be used for the national good in the short and long term (whether the peat was mined for fuel or not). The results of this phase were reported by Bjork in June 1984. He concluded that "without peat mining the Negril Morass would degrade still further". Peat extraction would open up unique possibilities for cooperation in the design and management of an ecologically diverse wetland, so the area could be changed from its present relatively homogeneous nature to "a mosaic of open water, islands and peninsulas … the area should be given the status of national park open for guided tourist tours".

The study concluded that fuel peat mining would open new possibilities at Negril for recreation and tourism (boating on the lake and organised guided tours), a restricted sport fishery, an extensive (but carefully managed) finfish fishery for local people, a shrimpery for local people, cage and pond aquaculture in parts of Lake Negril, and intensive aquaculture based on the production of shrimp, fish and crocodiles.

At one and the same time, Bjork concluded, peat mining as proposed would preserve the Negril Morass as a permanent wetland and "transform an environmental problem into an environmental asset with the creation of new jobs and an improved standard of living". An estimated 45-46 families would be able to earn a living from activities totally dependent on or closely related to the "environmental improvements" that came with fuel mining. Most of these would live off finfish fishing, shrimping and aquaculture; others would live off processing and the sport fishery.

Bjork contrasted the ecological quality of the Black River Lower Morass with the Negril Morass, pointing to the problems of erosion in the catchment area and loss of the Upper Morass (through agricultural development) as a settling basin. He maintained that the deposition of sediment was a serious threat to the Lower Morass as a wetland. Hence "ecologically careful" peat mining would "counteract the processes and activities otherwise leading to degradation of the environment" and would provide the basis not only for the permanent preservation of the Lower Morass as a wetland but would bring improvements in shrimp production and the preservation of endangered species, and make the wetland attractive as a national park [180].

The controversy over the scheme has attracted much local media attention, due in large part to Richard Perrott, a visiting research fellow at the University of the West Indies (UWI) and one of the key opponents of the scheme. In July 1984, William Saunders, Managing Director of PCJ, dismissed Perrott's evidence in support of his argument of environmental hazards as consisting of "tendentious half-truths, inaccuracies or outright nonsense; in short, pseudo-science designed to alarm the gullible" [181]. PCJ argued that rehabilitation of the Negril Swamp was not just necessary, but "mandatory" if the wetland ecosystem there was to be maintained; in the case of the Black River ecosystem, "it is mandatory that settling basins be provided for silt brought down through the Upper Morass".

The controversy has some unique features:

* The portfolio of the minister of mining and energy includes tourism. Minister Hugh Hart admits that the main motive for development is the economic return, but that if peat mining could be shown to have a serious impact on tourism or natural resources (such as fisheries) then he would not recommend its proceeding [182].

* The conservation and management of the Negril Swamp resources was made the responsibility of the PCJ after the visit to Negril of Prime Minister Seaga in December 1984. Mr Seaga also instructed PCJ to proceed with a wetlands national park which would preserve the Swamp Royal Palm Forest in the south of the Great Morass. These plans are now going ahead, but it is incongruous that the agency which is briefed to develop the peat resources of the morasses for energy is also responsible for conservation and environmental management of the same wetlands.

* The government agency responsible for natural resources policy — the NRCD — has played an increasingly minor role in the research project since its close involvement in the preliminary survey into the environmental consequences of the original proposals. The Department lacks both the budget and the personnel to carry out any effective ecological or environmental research — certainly nothing to match either PCJ or the Scandinavian Commission for Technical Cooperation. Its ability to continue to function as an effective conservation agency is questionable, yet NRCD has voiced major reservations about the peat mining project. Acting Director Beverly Miller prefers the "biological options" (i.e. protein and biomass production) to peat mining [183]. The department is particularly anxious to retain the "wetland nature of threatened systems rather than producing a highly lacustrine [lake] ecosystem of dubious manageability".

In the wake of growing controversy, ferocious exchanges in the press, public meetings called by PCJ and by the Negril Chamber of Commerce and appeals for an independent assessment from Sylvia Grizzle, chairman of the Peat Committee of the Negril Chamber of Commerce, an IUCN report attempted to identify the areas of environmental concern [184]. Its main findings:

*   PCJ have commissioned or carried out themselves an extensive and commendable range of environmental studies associated with peat mining proposals.
*   No alternative approaches to wetland rehabilitation, with the possibility of funding other than from peat mining for energy, have been reported in as much detail as the mining option.
*   The argument that the wetland mosaic produced by peat extraction would be ecologically more varied and productive and aesthetically more interesting than the existing Negril Morass currently dominated by sawgrass was unsatisfactory from a conservation standpoint. Otherwise there would be no case for maintaining blanket peats or any ecosystem of relatively low species diversity.
*   If eventually one lake results and replaces much of the existing Morass, it would become the largest single inland water body in Jamaica (about 15 sq km). The potential problems of managing this system cannot be underestimated. A model involving a controlled stratified seawater/freshwater system proposed by the Swedish consultants is still unproven. The single lake is vulnerable to damaging and unforeseen environmental effects (such as pollution) which would be more easily controlled in a number of smaller water bodies where varied uses can be separated.
*   There are still questions about the potential of the resource. Dr F. Brouers, Professor of Physics at UWI, criticises the Finnish project for being based on poor statistical analysis; "their results do not mention any errors; ... using the standard theories of statistical analysis, I can estimate the maximum lifetime of the (Negril) peat deposit exploitation to be 22 ± 4 years" [185]. If the reserve estimates prove overly optimistic after mining has started, one of two possibilities remain: the failure of the project to meet economic targets, or the need to develop reserves in areas previously set aside for conservation or other uses.
*   Relatively limited attention has been paid so far to the possible negative impacts of the project on the tourist industry (admittedly difficult to define exactly in Negril), which currently earns an estimated $25 million annually [186]. Development could certainly change the general ambience of a community whose world famous

11-km beach and crystal clear waters are prized for their tranquility. The power station would produce up to 52,000 tonnes of ash per year for 25-30 years. PCJ have been evaluating numerous site options and problems. Occasional plume emission and perhaps sulphurous odours are of concern to local residents. * There is even greater concern about the potential impact of heated effluent water from the cooling system of the power plant. It is generally agreed that many plants and animals in the tropics are already living close to their upper tolerance limits of temperature and that very small increases can have adverse effects [187]. Fine examples of coral reefs and seagrass beds occur along the coast which are not only valuable ecologically but are also an important and integral part of the tourist industry.

The Petroleum Corporation of Jamaica are well aware of such considerations. Raymond Anderson, who worked on the environmental impact studies of the Negril power plant for PCJ, pointed out the problem of thermal stress in this environment, emphasising the importance of outfall design and alignment to minimise the effects on benthic (bottom-dwelling) communities.

There is an indisputable finality in the physical extraction and burning of peat. By contrast, vegetation supported by the peat is a renewable resource. Using peat for energy forecloses alternative uses. The potential importance of these alternatives is not limited to conventional or proven uses, such as horticulture. Therapeutic preparations already used elsewhere, or biochemical products from peat extracts, may within a decade greatly increase the value of peat.

There are already possibilities of growing and harvesting Cladium (sawgrass) for biomass. In 1985, the University of Manchester's Institute of Science and Technology (UMIST) announced a prototype converter capable of turning plant material into oil. It has already been suggested that this might be a good use for sugar cane waste, a factor of particular interest to the Jamaican government, given the environmental problems of waste disposal from the sugar and rum production industry.

Peat mining consumes a finite energy resource in Jamaica, so it may not necessarily produce the best long-term advantage either to the environment or to the economy.

The ecological, environmental and socio-economic values of the Black River Lower Morass are considerably higher than those of Negril. Yet if mining goes ahead at Negril it may be more difficult to prevent mining in the Black River. There are bound to be unanticipated ecological problems, and no-one can suggest that the final outcome can be predicted with unqualified confidence. Indeed, the Bjork assessment points out that lessons will be learnt as mining proceeds. This is all right provided the problems are small, but it is a tantalisingly optimistic basis for development.

The IUCN report urges the Jamaican government to continue to take full account of the environmental implications of the scheme and to pursue the original NRCD/TGI proposal of looking into alternative energy and capitalisation schemes in similar depth. If mining does go ahead, it calls also for an independent environmental agency to be appointed to oversee the ecological and environmental aspects of development, to coordinate the scientific monitoring programme and to be responsible for the management and use of national park, nature reserve and wildlife sanctuary areas. One additional effect of the project may be a transfer of the *Cannabis* operation to the hillslopes and country east of the Negril Morass. This will lead to more deforestation, soil erosion and storm runoff — effects perhaps even more devastating than those of the current illicit operations in the Morass.

The initial findings of the IUCN report are now being reviewed with PCJ and other agencies in Jamaica.

The lessons from Jamaica

The Jamaican case has shown how strong local feeling can be in a Third World country about the exploitation of a non-renewable wetland resource, albeit in the apparent interests of the national economy.

But the people likely to be affected by the loss of an important buffer against intensive land use and degradation of environmental quality have needed independent scientific interpretations of the problems. While ecological and engineering feasibility studies may establish good investigative rapport, there is an implicit assumption that development will go ahead, but with agreed environmental guidelines.

The option of a complete rejection of the project on ecological grounds is clearly less likely. PCJ's dual involvement in development and conservation aspects of the project and the possible trade benefits of a go-ahead to donor countries has allowed local suspicions to proliferate. At a recent demonstration of experimental ponds in Negril to international peat scientists, a large fire started in the sawgrass. Dr Wade of PCJ pointed it out as a pertinent example of progressive destruction of the wetland; later it was suggested from other quarters (but has not been substantiated) that the fire may have been started deliberately — by whom or why is unknown.

The decision whether or not to proceed will be a political one, but development may depend on external funding from the World Bank, the Inter-American Bank or perhaps some European consortium.

If development does go ahead at Negril, then the ecologically much more valuable Black River Lower Morass is more likely to be mined.

More important, the technological developments pioneered in Jamaica may create a precedent, making it increasingly difficult to prevent rapid expansion of peat mining in important wetlands in North America, Africa, southeast Asia and throughout the Neotropics.

Negril may not be the finest tropical wetland (it is certainly not the most pristine) but it *is* a crucial economic and complex environmental test case.

Chapter 10

Social, economic and political conflicts

The battle to produce more food, reduce disease and raise standards of living have wiped out most of Europe's wetlands and many of those in the contiguous United States. Now the same forces threaten drastic change in the Third World.

It may seem hypocritical for environmental scientists from Northern countries which have squandered their wetlands to urge Third World governments to conserve their much larger tracts, rather than clearing them for farmland and urban development. But Northern scientists have the benefit of hindsight, which has given them a clearer scientific picture of the resources wasted when, for example, many of Britain's lowland marshes and the vast fens and marshland of the Great Kankakee swamp of Indiana and Illinois were drained. They see conservation not as an attempt to keep the Third World in their scenic mires, but as a means of safeguarding resources which can actually promote national development.

But it is hard to take this call seriously when many of the policies of Northern governments still actively encourage wetland destruction. Northern governments and public must first be convinced of the values of retaining wetlands, and begin to act on these convictions, before Third World policy-makers are likely to take much heed of the advice of Northern conservationists.

Developed countries have a major responsibility for determining the future of many of the world's tropical and sub-tropical wetlands. They often provide the expertise, funding and aid packages which affect — and often eliminate — these wetlands. Few Northern wetland scientists argue against the *use* of Southern wetlands. Most see it rather as their job to identify the real ecological wealth of these areas, and to work out ways of providing the greatest overall benefits on a sustained basis.

Of course, there are some 'uses' of wetlands that have nothing to do with the plans of either governments or scientists. Poaching and the cultivation of illegal drug plants are particular problems in relatively remote wetlands. Earlier this century, the illegal hunting of birds for plumage to satisfy the fashion market decimated bird populations in south Florida, where an Audubon Society warden was killed. (Yet the drama of this misuse did lead to a public outcry and was part of the pressure which led to the creation of the Everglades National Park.)

The value of wetland functions

The traditional view that there must be better uses for the land occupied by wetlands came about partly because swamps, marsh and bogs rarely *appeared* to contribute significantly to visible economic returns. But recent scientific research shows how misleading this appearance can be. Efforts to convince people of the worth of wetlands by actually calculating the economic values of wetland functions have shown that they more than earn their keep and their place in the landscape.

Eugene Odum, Professor of Ecology at the University of Georgia, US, puts the commercial and environmental value of coastal marsh in Georgia at $50,000-125,000 per hectare. The 'life support' value of saltmarsh (based on the conversion of solar energy) has similarly been put at $212,500 per hectare. Odum and his colleagues argued that a kilocalorie of solar energy converted into plant material in photosynthesis on a tidal marsh was no different to a kilocalorie of energy used in industrial production. Their figure is based on how much energy is used to produce one dollar of US Gross National Product. Compare this to the price of prime farmland in the United States, which may sell for $10,000 per hectare.

When proposals were made to drain the lower part of the Charles River near Boston, a biologist and an economist from Tufts University in Boston joined forces to work out the values of the lost wetland functions and their cost to replace. Their figures indicated that the wetland was worth 150 times more left intact, than if it were drained and sold for development.

	Value per hectare
Water supply	248,904
Flood prevention	82,457
Pollution reduction	60,955
Recreation and amenity	8,105
	————————
	$400,421

These figures put no costs on possible losses of species or future scientific values; there is no sure way of making such calculations. Yet the more concrete monetary values of wetland functions and costs of replacement with flood barriers, filter systems, water works and parks should prove both to the public and to politicians the financial worth of

Wetland type	Productivity (kg/sq m/year)
Cattail marsh (US)	5-6 (up to 15 reported)
Carex marsh (US)	2.7
Phragmites, Typha, Scirpus marsh (Czech)	1-2.7
Saltmarsh (US)	1-3
Saltmarsh (N. Europe)	0.8-1.2
Mangrove (Puerto Rico)	3
Swamp forest (US)	2-3
Seagrass (Thalassia) (US)	4.2
Bog, fen, muskeg (US/UK)	0.9
Midwest grassland (US)	0.5
Managed pasture (Australia)	2.8
Tropical rain forest	2-3
Pine forest	1
Cultivated land	0.7

Net primary productivity of wetlands and other ecosystems. Source: Newton, 1981.

these systems in terms of taxpayers' money.

Joseph Larson, Director of the Environmental Institute at the University of Massachusetts has made a thorough study of the various means of assessing wetland value. He concluded that attempts to put monetary values on the life support functions of wetlands came about because market economics do not "recognise that the primary productivity role that wetlands play in the ecosystem is related to human survival". Whatever the disagreements between scientists and economists regarding the validity of the approach, Larson says, "it appears that monetary valuation of wetlands is a tool that may have its main application in the political arena".

Society's slow response

Despite such calculations, the selling price of wetlands continues to be set not according to the value of their many services to society, but according to their financial value when converted to some other use. (The basic cost of the land is low; the cost of converting the wetland has always been a more important constraint to would-be developers.)

The wetlands system itself has been, and will continue to be, undervalued because there is no mechanism whereby the worth of wetlands to anyone but their owners can be evaluated. Our financial systems offer no way of calculating and totalling the value of wetland 'services' to people far from that wetland, perhaps even in other nations.

What motivation then, financial or otherwise, can be offered to private landowners or governments as landowners to persuade them to forego wetland destruction in the cause of 'economic development' because of the damage this destruction does to people outside the wetland? 'Education' may not be enough, nor may such exhortations as that found in US President Jimmy Carter's Environmental Message of 1977:

> "The lasting benefits that society derives from wetlands often far exceeds the immediate advantage their owners might get from draining or filling them. Their destruction shifts economic and environmental costs to other citizens ... who have no voice in the decision to alter them."

The economic and environmental costs in the African floodplains will centre on the loss of fisheries, loss of traditional grazing and loss of culture. For many species of plants and animals, some yet to be discovered, it means extinction. The global costs in terms of upsetting cycles of carbon dioxide and moisture are as yet impossible to calculate.

Governments remain reluctant to give wetlands the importance they deserve, for several reasons:

* Their ecological complexity means that there are many gaps in scientific understanding of how they work.
* Many wetlands are ephemeral systems which change naturally, and it is hard to relate that natural change to human alterations.
* Politicians are rarely gripped by the subject of wetlands.
* Politicians are loathe to admit responsibility for impacts beyond their own administrative or national boundaries. The acid pollution issue highlights such political reticence [189].

The reluctance is reflected in the slowness of many nations in signing the Ramsar convention. The United States, with its acknowledged lead in developing research, public awareness and protective legislation for wetlands, finally signed only in 1985, 14 years after the convention was opened for signature.

State support and subsidies

Despite the willingness of a growing number of politicians to speak out in favour of swamps and marshes, Northern governments continue to pay for the destruction of wetlands. They do this through state 'development' grants to landowners, public funding of major alteration projects, favourable tax structures and artificial price support for crops grown on reclaimed land.

In the United States, tax deductions and credits — together with US Department of Agriculture-guaranteed prices for crops grown on converted land — give farmers a major incentive to clear and drain wetlands. The government allows first year tax deductions of up to 25% of gross farm income for draining expenses, with amounts in excess of this recoverable in subsequent years. Further deductions are allowed on capital investments and interest payments incurred in drainage and clearing [190].

The Japanese government pays 80% of the cost of applying mineral topsoil to peat to farmers, who also receive support for drainage and fertiliser applications.

In Europe there has traditionally been enormous state and European Community support for farmers converting wetlands for more agricultural production. This means that European taxpayers pay to have the wetland converted, pay in various ways for the loss of wetland functions, and then pay subsidies and storage costs for the produce grown on the former wetland.

The Common Agricultural Policy (CAP) stimulates drainage by offering higher farm prices, increased export opportunities and attractive terms of financial support. France has the highest area of field drainage in Europe: 140,000 hectares per year. And of course land not actually drained for agricultural development may still suffer from agricultural development. The Camargue, France's most valued wetland, is under increasing threat, not from drainage itself but from runoff of agricultural land within and outside the regional park. Public funds meet 10-60% of the costs of field drainage, ditches and channels in France. Yet a 1979 report by the powerful statutory Social and Economic Council (CES) proposed an increase in the annual government support for drainage from $40 million (300 million francs) to $136 million (one billion francs). In 1981, $21 million (151 million francs) was paid out in public subsidies for field drainage and ditches alone [191].

The influence of this type of policy in accelerating or causing wetland loss is undeniable. The Marais des Echets, part of Les Domes (near Lyons in eastern France), was drained in the 1960s and 1970s with public funding. Some 40% of the coastal wetlands of Brittany have disappeared in the last 20 years, and two-thirds of the remainder are seriously affected by drainage and similar activities [192]. Some 80% of the marshes of the Landes de Gascogne in southwest France, an extremely important habitat for migratory crane, have been drained.

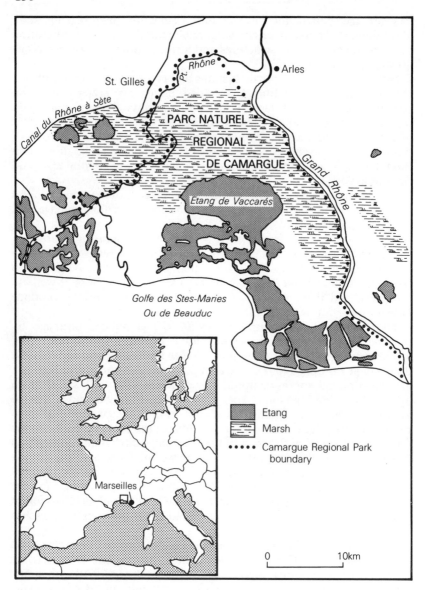

St. Gilles

Arles

Pt. Rhône

Canal du Rhône à Sète

PARC NATUREL

REGIONAL

DE CAMARGUE

Grand Rhône

Etang de Vaccarés

Golfe des Stes-Maries
Ou de Beauduc

Marseilles

▨ Etang

▤ Marsh

•••• Camargue Regional Park
boundary

0   10km

The Camargue of southeast France.

A report by the Office National de la Chasse (National Hunting Office) revealed that nearly half of the 25 wetlands of major importance for waterfowl had already been adversely affected by agricultural drainage [193]. About 600,000 hectares of wetland in France are at risk from planned agricultural drainage [194]. Environmental impact studies became mandatory in 1976 for schemes costing more than $825,000 (6 million francs) in a year. However, most wetland drainage programmes are scheduled over several years, so even the most expensive schemes can fall below the limit [195].

Because of its many wetlands and mild winter, Ireland is an important wintering area for waterfowl. About 70% of the entire Greenland race of the white-fronted goose (*Anser albifrons*) winter there, mainly on the Wexford Slobs in southeast Ireland. But again, the state is supporting the destruction of the nation's wetlands. Between 1949 and 1979, the state paid $440 million (IR£350 million) for land reclamation and field drainage. Major drainage has been funded entirely by the government for the last 30 years, and up to 70% of field drainage costs may be met by the state [196].

Since it became a member of the European Community (EC), Ireland has also received major EC grants and loans for large-scale drainage works such as the Western Drainage Scheme in the northwest, started in 1979. With subsidies from both Brussels and Dublin, drainage costs to farmers have fallen by 40%. Not surprisingly, this has encouraged rapid development [197]. More than $3.75-8.75 million (IR£3-7 million) was spent on grants for field drainage in 1981, amounting to $375 (IR£300) per hectare.

Drainage of the Boyne River tributaries west of Dublin has reduced wetland habitats, fish productivity and particularly salmon numbers. Against little effective opposition from conservation groups, many of the unique 'turloughs' (shallow temporary lakes) in the area have been destroyed. This may eventually lead to the extinction of black-necked grebe as a breeding species in Ireland. There are plans to drain parts of the Shannon River catchment area, despite its five wetland sites of international importance. Some 80,000 hectares of bog have been drained since 1946, leaving only about 5% in their original state. A 1983 European parliament report warns that "the unique ecosystems of the Irish bogs will vanish completely in the next five years unless effective preventative measures are taken very soon."

The lack of concern for wetland environments on the part of the Irish government, particularly in provisions associated with the Western Drainage Scheme, has caused some friction with the EC. This stems from token EC attempts to protect wetlands through the inclusion of 'environmental clauses' in the regulations for stimulating agriculture in poorer western areas. The EC has concluded that "unless the Irish government displays much greater determination in conserving wetlands, the prospects of further arterial drainage work, particularly in the Shannon catchment, can only be interpreted as a major threat to the environment" [198].

Between the early 1800s and 1939, 4.7 million hectares — an area larger than Denmark — of agricultural land in England and Wales were drained [199]. State subsidies have accelerated the decline in wetlands since the Second World War, when 50% drainage grants were introduced. Half the country's inland wetlands have been adversely affected since 1949. The losses include 20,000 hectares of saltmarsh and mudflats in The Wash reclaimed for agriculture in the last 30 years. Grazing marshes once covered 1.5 million hectares in England and Wales; only small areas now remain [200].

The area of field drained by sub-surface drainage has increased from 10-15,000 hectares per year in the 1940s to about 120,000 ha/year today. Farmers were given £60 million in grants for field drainage in 1982, with levels of government assistance varying from 50-70% of costs.

The loss and fragmentation of grazing marsh habitat has been a primary cause of the decline in numbers of breeding waterfowl in northern Kent [201]. Romney Marsh in the southeast was 7% arable in 1931, but is now over 50% arable, with 500 hectares being converted annually throughout the 1960s. In the uplands, there has been drainage and reclamation of moorland.

Increases in agricultural productivity through drainage, fertiliser application and conversion of grazing marshland to arable land in wetland catchments have been a major factor in changes in the Norfolk Broads apparent from the 1960s. Eutrophication of Broads waters has caused fish kills, increased botulism (a bacterial infection) in birds, the elimination of aquatic plants and a general loss of animal life through the decline in water quality.

"Improvement schemes threaten nearly all of the remaining ornithologically important wet lowland grassland in England and Wales", warns the Royal Society for the Protection of Birds [202], one of Britain's biggest and most active conservation groups. Britain's system of state support for wetland drainage has clashed directly with the objectives of the Nature Conservancy Council and national parks (funded from other arms of government). Since the implementation of the 1981 Wildlife and Countryside Act, government agricultural advisors are required to make farmers aware of their legal obligations to preserve important habitats, including wetlands.

Southwest England has been a major testing ground for the gradual change in attitudes which must come if some of the last remaining British wetlands are to be preserved. The conflicts between agricultural intensification and wetland conservation have been acrimonious, both in the upland peatlands of Exmoor and the lowland grazing marshes and peats of the Somerset Levels. So bitter has been the argument in West Sedgemoor (Somerset) that effigies of conservationists were hanged and burnt there in 1983.

There is no longer automatic grant support for activities which degrade important wetland or moorland sites. But, in protected areas, if an application for a grant is turned down on conservation grounds, then the farmer must be offered a management agreement which compensates him for potential lost income. So the cost of conservation is still greatly inflated by the artificially high prices under the EC's Common Agricultural Policy. The major absurdity in this system is that some farmers may still be encouraged to lodge development plans in the hope of receiving compensation for not doing something that, did such a system not exist, they may not want to do in the first place. Conversely, and somewhat ironically, the very survival of many wetland types in Europe depends on the maintenance of *traditional* agricultural techniques. For example, low intensity grazing prevents encroachment by woody species in bogs and marshes. In such cases, management agreements which support those traditional techniques can help conserve wetlands.

Disease eradication

The threat of disease long kept people out of wetlands, discouraged their use and preserved their integrity. More recently, eradication of disease has been used as an argument for the eradication of wetlands.

In 1827, many people were still "fearful of entering the fens of Cambridgeshire, least the Marsh Miasma should shorten their lives" [203]. These were not unreasonable fears, for malaria (from the Italian 'mala aria', or bad air) was still prevalent in eastern England and throughout Europe in the early 19th Century. It was attributed to the 'miasma' (unhealthy odours) and germs produced by the action of the sun on decomposing vegetation alternately covered and uncovered by water [204]. The eradication of the disease before the end of the 19th Century was generally attributed to better drainage; this undoubtedly coloured attitudes towards marshland and swamp, not only in Europe but wherever in the world Europeans came into contact with wet, disease-ridden environments.

In fact, improved sanitation and housing were probably more important. Indeed, the *Anopheles* mosquito, which carries malaria in malarial regions, is still found in areas of remaining marsh in Europe [205]. Realisation that wetlands were not the direct source of disease, but were the habitat for many parasites and disease vectors such as mosquitoes and snails, simply confirmed the view that drainage was essential. Some drainage schemes have been aimed mainly at eradicating disease or controlling pests. The drainage of wet meadows in Britain to combat sheep liver fluke (snail-carried) and the excavation of ditches in saltmarshes along the eastern coast of the United States to control mosquitoes are two examples. The US ditching efforts of the 1930s and 1940s were unsuccessful because they barely affected the shallow depressions in the marshes where mosquitoes laid eggs.

More recent open marsh water management, in which denser systems of connecting ditches eliminate these depressions, has been much more successful, particularly in New Jersey, Maryland and Delaware. But there are ecological costs. Where the ditches allow tidal flushing, species such as saltmeadow hay (*Spartina patens*) and spikegrass (*Distichlis spicata*) have been replaced by sea myrtle (*Baccharis halinifolia*) and marsh elder (*Iva frutscens*). This has reduced the habitat for waterfowl and marshland animals [206].

The reduction of mosquito breeding areas was one motive for draining the Hula papyrus swamp in northern Israel in the 1950s (although the primary motive was agricultural development). The result was serious ecological and environmental damage. Only 310 hectares of the original 5,000-hectare swamp were preserved for drainage, in a country where efforts to establish successful agriculture have left little room for conservation. Almost all 12,000 hectares of the other swamps which existed in the country at the turn of the century were drained between 1920 and 1940. Papyrus probably reaches its northern limits in the Hula Swamp Nature Reserve, and northern species like bracken (*Pteridium aquilinum*) and white water lily (*Nymphaea alba*) are at their southern limit [207].

Casualties of the Hula Swamp drainage include several plants and over 30% of the original nesting bird species. Five bird species have disappeared completely from Israel, almost certainly because drainage elsewhere gave them no alternative sites [208].

In some cases, draining wetlands to control disease-carrying pests can actually increase the numbers of those pests. The two *Anopheles* mosquitoes mainly responsible for malaria in Uganda breed at the edge of the swamplands, where shallow, fluctuating and stagnant water provides the ideal habitat. Conditions deeper in the swamps are unsuitable. However, drainage can increase the overall area of the small, shallow and ephemeral water bodies the mosquitoes prefer. These may be in surface irregularities of the drained swamp or in poorly maintained ditches and irrigation systems, effectively increasing the 'edge effect'.

New health risks. Sudanese farmers know only too well the debilitating effects of schistosomiasis (bilharzia), which has expanded along the Nile with the increase of irrigation channels.

The planned expansion of irrigated agriculture on floodplains throughout Africa, such as the current schemes in the valley of the Senegal River, is likely to increase mosquito breeding sites and the populations of the snails which carry schistosomiasis. The construction of reservoirs in Sri Lanka has increased the spread of malaria, and irrigation in Thailand has increased the problem of human liver fluke. The black flies which carry river blindness (onchocersiasis) prefer fast-flowing water to slow canal water, and the tailrace waters below dams have locally increased numbers of these flies [208a].

Under natural conditions, when floodplains dry out during the dry season, the disease organisms and their carriers die out or leave. This is precisely the time when people are sowing crops or letting their livestock graze in the area. Irrigation ditches and reservoirs may provide year-round use for the disease vectors and organisms, and may increase disease. Such effects ought to be investigated — and remedies decided — before schemes proceed.

The threat of pesticides

The spraying of pesticides such as DDT is an alternative to draining wetlands, but it has its own costs — some obvious, some not so obvious:

* the chemicals and the spraying are themselves expensive;
* insects can rapidly develop disease resistance, so that pesticides that are more expensive, and more dangerous to humans, must be used;
* pesticides build up in food chains and can expose higher organisms — birds and mammals — to lethal doses. Many of the target organisms can develop resistant strains necessitating the continuous development of new chemicals.

The buildup of biocides or their chemical derivatives through the food chain exposes higher organisms to harmful and often lethal doses. At Clear Lake, California, insecticide (chlorinated hydrocarbon DDD) was sprayed in 1949 in an attempt to control the number of gnats. The first application eliminated 99% of the population and so did a second application in 1954. By the time the lake was sprayed for a third time in 1957, the gnat and 150 species of insects and other pests had developed some immunity to the pesticide. Within two weeks of each spraying, no chemical could be detected in the lake waters — it had all been assimilated by living organisms.

The first signs of ecological damage appeared in 1950. Prior to this, Clear Lake had been a nesting ground for about 1,000 pairs of western grebes. In 1960 there were only 30 pairs left [209]. Between 1950 and

1961 no young were produced. Many adults died soon after the 1954 and 1957 sprayings and in subsequent years. In 1962 a single grebe hatched and reproduction success was poor until 1969. The lake plankton contained 250 times the concentration of the original application of pesticide, frogs 2,000 times the concentration in their visceral fat, and the grebes 80,000 times.

This concentration through the food chain exposes the organisms least able to cope with the toxins to the highest doses, and also explains why insecticides are quickly undetectable in the lake waters alone.

Thus both draining or spraying harm wetland ecosystems directly, while spraying can open the wetland area up for conversion to farming. Governments must carefully weigh up the health, welfare and social benefits of removing one disease threat against the environmental, economic and other possible disease threats.

Plans to eradicate tsetse fly from the Okavango delta in Botswana have promoted more intensive cattle grazing there. A game fence has been built around much of the delta to conserve wetland for wildlife, stop the spread of foot and mouth disease from game to valuable livestock, and prevent overgrazing [210]. (The Veterinary Cordon Fences are only on the southern and eastern flanks of the delta region, so do not completely impede wild animal movements in and out of the wetland.)

The success of the scheme relies heavily on the maintenance of the fence, the cooperation of local inhabitants, and lack of side-effects from chemical spraying. Botswana has much to lose if the management fails: access to the highly profitable European beef market, a lucrative and growing tourist industry with wildlife safaris alone worth nearly $15 million [211], and a most important and unique ecological resource.

Chapter 11

Politics, people and foreign aid

Agriculture is not the only motive for draining or altering wetlands.

The reclamation of nearly two-thirds of the peatland on Japan's Hokkaido island earlier this century was important in strengthening Japan's political hold on the recently colonised prefecture. In Israel, the strategic importance of establishing permanent settlement and agriculture overrides any possibility of maintaining large areas of swamp, especially in the politically sensitive zones close to the Lebanese and Syrian borders.

Personal ambitions too have led to wetland conversion. In 1575, Peter Morris applied for a patent to manufacture equipment in England's Fenland "to drain waters above their natural level and to drayne waterishe and mooreishe grounds" [212]. Cornelius Vermuyden of the Netherlands, with his "great designe" of drainage networks in the 17th Century, exemplifies the ambitions which, over 300 years, have transformed one of Europe's largest wetland mosaics into a landscape of intense cultivation.

Three of the founding fathers of America — George Washington, Thomas Jefferson and Patrick Henry — formed a company in 1763 to drain the Great Dismal Swamp in Virginia and North Carolina for agriculture. Ironically, the family of William Bartram, one of America's first naturalists, profited from the grain yields of some of the wetlands they drained, although the overall plan to convert the area into rich farmland itself failed. The ploughing and agricultural reclamation of moorland on Exmoor in England — which was to become such a sensitive conservation and political issue in the 1970s and 1980s — was begun over a century before by John Knight, caught up in the enthusiasm of the 19th Century agricultural revolution and determined to carve out a productive agricultural estate.

The roles of individuals are being played today by large corporate agricultural operations, financial and investment institutions, farmers, development and engineering consultancies, aid agencies and government departments. Direct profit is an obvious goal, but wetlands are often sacrificed on the altars of political ambition and speculative investment, and by intransigent administrative systems.

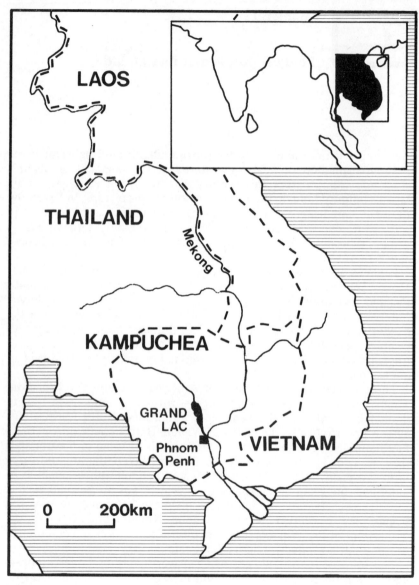

The Mekong delta.

**More food, fewer imports,
and a better standard of living**

The political debate over Third World wetlands usually boils down to a straight choice of either:

1. turning them over to short-term direct food production, high density aquaculture or intensive livestock rearing (or using them to make foreign currency savings through peat mining or commercial wood production); or
2. conserving them for long-term economic, ecological and environmental reasons.

Conservation usually loses out, overidden by the clamour for direct and immediate economic benefits. The Fijian ministry of agriculture, for example, is well aware of the importance of the country's coastal wetlands, particularly to fisheries. But it feels that the need to increase home-produced rice is too great to prevent agricultural development of the Rewa delta and other residual coastal swamps [213].

"We cannot afford not to develop" is a common argument, used not only by politicians but also by environmentalists in the Third World. It is epitomised in the environmental programme for the development of the lower basin of the Mekong, southeast Asia's largest river. The assumption is that the environment is globally stable and that ecological systems have considerable internal resilience; they can tolerate major disturbances and recover when the disturbances are removed. The environmental policy of the Mekong Committee, charged with overseeing the development of the delta (see Chapter 12), hinges on the premise that "big is necessary", because poor developing countries "have no vested interest in constancy, if only because the *status quo* does not serve well the hopes and aspirations of a majority of their people; it also does not cater to their basic needs" [214].

The policy in the Mekong is not to protect the basin's natural environment *per se* but to ensure that the overall productivity of natural resources is not harmed by development, that environmental functions are integrated into development projects for maximum social and economic benefit, and that the potential for development is not undermined by planning mistakes.

The Environmental Unit formed by the Mekong Committee in 1976 was a major step forward in ensuring that continued development would not bring ecological destruction to the highly interdependent wetlands of the Mekong. The Unit does not actually *prevent* development; its aim is to ensure that measures are taken which will *reduce* the adverse ecological consequences of development. Particular attention is being paid to the status of Mekong fisheries (in the delta alone they returned a

Type of operation	US$/ha/year		
	Gross value of production	Cash expenditure	Net return
Wetland aquaculture			
Open wetlands	300	50	250
Cages in wetlands	1,370,000	1,038,000	232,000
Pens in wetlands	14,000	6,600	7,400
Agriculture			
Broadcast rice (native)	115	43	72
Transplant rice (native)	191	59	132
High yielding rice (dry)	365	165	200
High yielding rice (wet)	365	148	217
Tobacco	337	101	236
Chewing cane	734	167	567
Tomato	396	98	298
Sweet corn	306	107	119
Cucumber	308	69	239
Mung beans	118	30	88
Field corn	203	100	103
Soya beans	193	90	103
Peanut	360	106	254
Cotton	448	178	270
Jute	214	69	145
Miscellaneous vegetables	412	26	386
Fruits	350	16	334

Estimated costs and benefits for wetland aquaculture and agricultural operations in the Mekong basin. Source: Pantulu 1981, adapted from Mekong Committee (1975) and Pantulu (1972, 1979).

catch of 520,000 tonnes in 1980, worth $200 million), and to the importance of inundation to the planned large-scale agricultural development of the Nam Songkhram basin, which will seriously affect fisheries [215].

This concept of 'mitigation' is unpopular with wetland ecologists, except as a last resort. Third World planners too rarely ask themselves whether investment would be better directed to improving production on existing farmland (or in other economic sectors), rather than disrupting wetland ecosystems which, even after reclamation, are often more difficult or expensive to manage for large-scale economic agriculture. Rumania provides an example applicable to the Third

World. Professor Pons of the Agricultural University at Wageningen in the Netherlands, argues that the Rumanian economy and environment would benefit more by the improvement of existing cultivated land than by plans to reclaim 125,000 hectares and double the local population of the Danube delta. The soils of the delta are unsuited for intensive agriculture, and the area supports important breeding populations of white pelican (*Pelecanus onocrotalus*), dalmatian pelican (*Pelecanus crispus*) and pygmy cormorant (*Phalacrocorax pygmaeus*) [216].

The question applies also to current proposals to develop the Mekong's water and land resources. Agricultural development and intensified management of the wetland is complicated in several ways. Nearly half the delta (about 1.8 million hectares) has acid sulphate soils which can acidify the water draining off them. The elevation of the land creates drainage problems, flooding brings periodic inundation, and there is the danger of salt water intrusion. Discharge in low-flow periods is too low to provide enough water for irrigation. And agricultural and other developments pose a serious threat to fisheries and wildlife resources.

The 1985 Mekong Committee mission to Vietnam [217] proposed substantial environmental monitoring, but left three areas out of its recommendations: fisheries, mangroves and wildlife. The first is particularly worrying in view of the size of the catch and the dependency on fishing of many millions of people. The Mekong Secretariat fully admits that there could be "considerable adverse effects" to the fisheries from agricultural and other development. But evaluation of the scale of the impact needs detailed monitoring; there are no provisions for this yet because of "the magnitude of inputs" (i.e. money, time and personnel) needed to carry them out. "However," says the report, "as in the case of mangroves and wildlife conservation [by implication clearly recognised as important and vulnerable resources], separate fishery studies projects could be formulated if the Government of Vietnam so desires."

It can only be hoped that the Vietnam government, the Mekong Committee, UNEP, the Dutch government and others involved in the delta development programme do 'so desire'. There is much more chance of high productivity in an intact wetland ecosystem than in delicately poised acid sulphate soils. The immediate yields from the agro-ecosystem may be higher but they do not amount to a certain long-term investment.

Ireland's Bord na Mona argues that any ecological damage caused by its peat mining is a small price to pay for the benefits of reduced fuel import bills and an improved standard of living. The same argument features prominently in Jamaica's plans to mine the Negril and Black River peat morasses (see Chapter 9). Nearly all (98%) of Jamaica's fuel needs are met by oil imports, accounting for nearly a fifth of the country's annual import bill. When the government set up the Petroleum Corporation of Jamaica (PCJ) in 1979, it gave it a mandate to develop new sources of energy, including as far as possible indigenous resources. Only in this way, argues mining and energy minister Hugh Hart, can Jamaica counter increasing energy prices, increasing costs of hard currency, and fluctuating international market conditions.

Hart is confident that using the peat for electricity generation would yield at least 90 megawatts annually for 25-30 years (or more than 35% of present consumption); make foreign exchange savings of $24 million a year; allow a transition period for the development of alternative indigenous energy resources and more favourable arrangements for fuel imports; stabilise energy prices; create new industries fuelled by peat energy; and establish other peat-related industries (such as horticulture peat production).

The decision whether or not to mine the peat may not be made for a number of years. By that time, more detailed knowledge of the benefits that *might* result from a similar investment in renewable energy (e.g. solar power or biogas) or in another sector of the economy, such as tourism, might be available. Sectors of the Negril tourist industry are currently against the energy project. But the tourism argument may collapse altogether when a power station and the associated industrial and social infrastructure is built. Jamaica and the technical and financial advisers must all be absolutely certain that the peat mining project is the best long-term option for the nation's economy.

Controlling landowners

Governments — even those under pressure from the conservation lobby — generally find it hard to prevent the development of land traditionally regarded as unproductive, especially where it is privately owned and the owners may be realising long held personal ambitions. The only wetlands that can be protected with any reasonable certainty are those bought outright for conservation or subjected to strict planning controls — but even these can be affected by activities elsewhere in the catchment or tidal zone.

It would cost an estimated $7.5 million to buy just the more important examples of bog habitat in Britain [218]. Because of the financial constraints on most private and government conservation agencies, more and more wetlands in Europe and North America are being protected through lease and management agreements. But although the initial costs are much less than outright purchase, they mount up, and usually have to be renegotiated after 5-10 years. There has to be a dramatic increase in funds or a switch in subsidy policy if any more areas are to be protected.

There is evidence of such a switch beginning in Europe. Britain's Ministry of Agriculture, Fisheries and Food won EC backing in 1985 to grant aid to the traditional agricultural practices needed to maintain the wetland environment of the Norfolk Broads, rather than aid intensification and ecologically damaging projects. The costs have to be met for the time being from the British Treasury rather than Brussels, but the change is a great political success. The EC does not readily respond to innovation [219]. For management agreements to work, landowners must adhere strictly to guidelines agreed with the appropriate conservation agency. Initial monitoring schemes are essential because of the difficulty of deciding exactly what levels of land use activities the system can tolerate.

A monitoring programme in Britain's Exmoor National Park has examined the soil and vegetation changes brought by agreed levels of lime application and stocking rates over an eight-year period [220]. After an initial sharp rise in alkalinity and microbial activity (which in the long term would increase peat oxidation and change the character of the wet upland soils and acid tolerant vegetation), the soil is gradually returning to normal. So the moorland plant community will not be invaded by a more nutrient-demanding and agriculturally productive flora.

The real value of this type of research will be to work out a way of improving a farmer's production (thereby minimising the costs to the taxpayer of a management agreement) while staying within the ecosystem's buffering capability, and using the 'natural' vegetation rather than an artificially reseeded one. But this kind of research cannot be completed in 1-3 years, the normal range for research grants and contracts. Scientific studies need to run for a decade or more if we are to learn how to manage wetlands properly, ensure their survival, and make sure that society enjoys the full benefit of wetlands. Research councils and environmental agencies are usually against such long-term commitments, and in the highly competitive realms of scientific peer review and diminishing funds, such longer term proposals generally do not fare well.

The US National Science Foundation (NSF), however, has seen some light. Its Long Term Ecological Research (LTER) programme acknowledges that some ecological phenomena unfold over decades or centuries, and that long-term trends in natural ecosystems have rarely been monitored systematically. Sites selected for more careful study include a wide range of ecosystems, from the marshes and swamps of the Okefenokee National Wildlife Refuge in Georgia to the riverine marsh, floodplain forest and aquatic communities of the Illinois and

Upper Mississippi River. This type of commitment from national and international funding agencies must be extended to key sites throughout the world, especially in Brazil, Africa and parts of southeast Asia where development pressures are growing rapidly and sustainable management strategies are needed.

Expertise, funding and foreign aid

Most of the civil engineering and land projects causing removal or disruption of wetlands in the Third World (and some even in developed countries) are being backed by foreign expertise and funding, and frequently by aid packages.

The impact of exported expertise has a long history. In the 17th Century the Dutchmen Peter Morris, Humphrey Bradley, William Mostart and Cornelius Vermuyden came to England to drain the fens and marshes of Essex, Cambridgeshire and the Thames [221]. Three hundred years later, Dutch authorities such as the Department of Public Works, the Lake Ijssel Development Authority, the government service for land and water use and the International Institute for Land Reclamation and Improvement play a key role in the planning and implementation of dam, polder and drainage projects all over the world.

Dutch engineering companies have been involved in more than half the 180 large polder projects carried out or planned in the last 20 years [222]. They have been particularly active in the African floodplains (e.g. the Tana delta, the Kafue River and the Jonglei Canal scheme) and in southeast Asia, especially in the Mekong basin. The Netherlands government contributes significant financial assistance through bilateral or international aid programmes. "The realisation and exploitation phase is especially important to Dutch contractors and suppliers" say W.G. Braakhekke, of the Dutch Society for the Protection of Birds, and C.A. Drijver, of the Centre of Environmental Studies at the University of Leiden. Out of about 180 larger polder projects, they point out, in only nine cases (5%) can it be said that a serious study was made of the consequences of reclamation for the natural values and functions of the area.

Braakhekke and Drijver point out that a Dutch-financed survey led to the recommendation that the construction of irrigation areas, dykes and polders on the floodplains of Zambia's Kafue River should be further investigated. It was a Dutch team that studied the feasibility of draining Jamaica's Black River Morasses for agriculture in 1967 and 1974. The reclamation project in the Upper Morass is now being developed by the Black River Upper Morass Development Company (BRUMDEC) with loan finance from the Inter-American Development Bank (IDB).

Donor or exporting nations, especially those that are signatories to the Ramsar convention, have an obligation to take account of possible ecological and environmental impacts — *in the first stage of survey and planning, not when decisions are taken and ways of investigating the effects are being sought.* The responsibility should not rest solely with the recipient country. This is an approach endorsed by the 1980 Cagliari meeting of Ramsar nations which called for wetland development to be allowed only when all the relevant issues had been weighed, and for particular attention to be paid to conservation in collaborative projects with developing countries.

Much aid has been given to — and is being sought by — the developing countries engaged in wetland conversion to carry out environmental studies. The Petroleum Corporation of Jamaica now proposes to establish a national park over 81 hectares of Swamp Royal Palm (*Roystonea princeps*) and adjacent sedge wetland in Negril. Some of the funding for the scheme may be sought from USAID and other international agencies. One of the aims of the proposed development is "to demonstrate the possibility of enhancing degraded tropical wetlands". The plan for a 'recreational lake' including islands is very similar to a scaled-down version of the post-peat mining landscape proposed for the larger part of the Negril Morass.

The Lower Mekong Basin Committee has been particularly active in securing support for its environmental programmes and has many projects awaiting funding. Commitment like this is welcome, but it is vital that these and other assessments are timed so that the results can have real influence on political decisions.

It seems at times that developed nations may be queuing up to help in the conversion of wetlands to other uses. While the Dutch played a key role in the reclamation of 2,000 hectares of the Black River Upper Morass for agricultural development, the Japanese government has agreed recently to a request from Jamaica to assess the feasibility of reclaiming a further 3,000 hectares of the Lower Morass for rice cultivation.

The pre-feasibility report [223] contains a brief environmental assessment, which points out (*Inter alia*) that 80% of *Typha* hummocky swamp and *Cladium-Sagittaria* association would be turned into paddy in the Broad River basin. It also warns of the vulnerability of the unique aquatic vegetation of the Broad River and its attractive blue holes (springs of the Styx and Broad/Cashoo rivers) to reduced water quality and far-reaching hydrological changes, and the possible loss of wildlife habitat and important fisheries. But there is no suggestion that these changes might be so significant that the US$38 million development should not go ahead, although conservation of important habitats is advocated strongly.

The projected annual benefit (at full economic development) of some US$5.8 million derived from the scheme may well seem appealing, but may be considerably reduced if a shrinking peat surface produces inflated water management costs. Meanwhile, the ecological costs of lost natural habitat and functions, and a possible decline in the harvest of natural shrimp (itself worth some US$550,000 a year) and in fishery resources may indicate that even the economics are not attractive in the longer term.

Chapter 12
Wetland management:
problems and cures

The survival of wetlands depends on protection, but it may depend more on management. Agreeing that sustained productivity and wetland maintenance are desirable is one thing; actually achieving these goals is quite another. The ecological characteristics of wetlands pose particular problems, best illustrated at two different levels: the international and the national.

International problems of wetland management

Because wetlands are natural systems, their boundaries do not neatly follow national frontiers. The Sundarbans is shared by Bangladesh and India, the Gran Pantanal by Brazil, Paraguay and Bolivia. More frequently, the rivers or other hydrological driving forces that feed a wetland may rise hundreds or thousands of kilometres from the wetland itself, often crossing several administrative, political or international boundaries.

The problem is particularly acute in Africa. Baturiya, a proposed wetland game reserve in the Hadejia River Valley, Nigeria, has one of the best surviving examples of Sahelian floodplain woodland. Its survival depends not just on controlling the grazing of local Fulani cattle but on the advent of years sufficiently wet to overcome the reduction in river flow caused by offtake of water upstream. There has been no flood for two years.

Dr Patrick Dugan, Wetlands Programme Officer for IUCN, concludes that the case "is but one of many examples of the problems of water management currently faced by the states of northern Nigeria and their Sahelian neighbours. Without improved coordination among water users, the long-term future for the water resource and the people dependent upon this is bleak" [224]. Discussions are now being held to explore ways and means by which the Nigerian states of Kano and Borno can collaborate on the establishment of cross-border wetland reserves — including Baturiya — which bring benefits to people and wildlife.

Lake Chad poses larger problems. Between April 1984 and January

1985, the water edge receded 40 km in the Nigerian sector; by March 1985 there was virtually no water left [225]. Poor rainfall is only part of the explanation. Lake Chad is fed mainly by the Logone and Chari rivers in Cameroon, from which major dams are now diverting water to large-scale irrigation projects. "If Lake Chad is ever to return to some semblance of the area covered in the late 1970s", notes Dugan, "the whole water regime of the Chad basin ... needs to be reviewed and corrective measures taken." Whether this is possible, he notes, depends on the extent to which the catchment states — Nigeria, Niger, Chad and Cameroon — can be persuaded of the need to treat the waters of the Chad basin as an international resource, and of the long-term benefits of doing so [226]. The alternative is continued ecological, economic and human disaster. A major irrigation scheme run by the Chad Basin Rural Development Authority on the southern part of the Nigerian lakeshore yielded no crops in 1984/85; the government investment of $230 million looks increasingly ill-advised.

An IUCN mission to Borno state, Nigeria, in 1985 established that the federal Ministry of Agriculture and Natural Resources was aware of — and concerned by — the wetland problems of the region. Indeed, Permanent Secretary Imbrahim Musa was especially concerned by the "need for greater inter-state and international agreement on the management of the water supply to the wetland areas and of the agriculture, grazing and fishing dependent upon these" [227].

Many of the world's finest surviving wetlands — and the people who depend on them — face similar threats from the external control of water supplies. Angola controls the water supply to Botswana's Okavango swamps. The Sundarbans forest has been progressively deteriorating over the last decade as the dry-season flow down the Ganges has been cut by barrages, irrigation and groundwater abstraction [228]. Recent agreement between India and Bangladesh has increased the dry-season flow of freshwater but observers doubt whether economic developments based on freshwater resources will pay heed to protection of the Sundarbans, despite widespread recognition of their international importance to coastal fisheries.

General awareness needs to be translated into management and protection strategies that actually work. There are two main routes to achieving this: establishing bodies to control, or at least influence, the management and development of internationally shared or dependent wetlands, and convincing governments and the public of the value of the sustainable development of wetlands.

Multinational wetland management

The Mekong Basin. In 1957, the governments that share the Mekong (Laos, Kampuchea, Thailand and Vietnam) established the Committee for Coordination of Investigations of the Lower Mekong Basin. The basin covers an area of more than 600,000 sq km, and supports a population of 40 million. Resource development in the Lower Mekong is managed by the Committee, whose major goal is to encourage the development of hydroelectric power, agriculture and industry alongside sensible environmental management.

The overriding environmental dictate for shared water resource projects — according to Dr Pantulu, Chief of the Environmental Unit in the Mekong Secretariat — is the traditional concept of river rights: a user must provide downstream a specific amount of water of a quality not less than that of the original supply. The Committee is bound by its statutes to allow development only with the unanimous support of all the member countries. The Secretariat actually carries out the tasks agreed by the Committee and its work is funded by the member countries, by the UN Development Programme and by foreign aid packages.

The Environmental Unit was set up in 1976 to incorporate environmental concerns in the basin development programme. There are two stages in its work. First, it carries out environmental assessment and management studies — ecological studies, sectoral studies (e.g. impact on fisheries, wildlife and public health) and assessments of the environmental impact of projects such as dam construction. A study of the effects of possible additional dam sites upstream of the Nam Ngum reservoir in Laos revealed that one site might have a serious effect on water quality, leading to drastic effects on the highly productive fisheries of the existing reservoir — worth $1.4 million a year.

Second, it carries out pilot development, management and rehabilitation schemes to train local managers and to put its theories to the test. Many of the Mekong schemes are aimed at maintaining and developing key fisheries resources. This includes augmenting natural production, and reintroducing or rehabilitating fish species threatened or seriously affected by development projects. There is particular concern for the survival of the freshwater prawn, *Macrobrachium rosenbergii*, which seasonally migrates for spawning from freshwater areas of the Mekong to the estuaries.

The Mekong approach provides a good example to other schemes in that wetland ecosystems are treated in their whole environmental context. This is vital, because changes in other areas and in often very different ecosystems elsewhere in a catchment can have just as drastic an effect as if the wetland itself were directly altered. According to

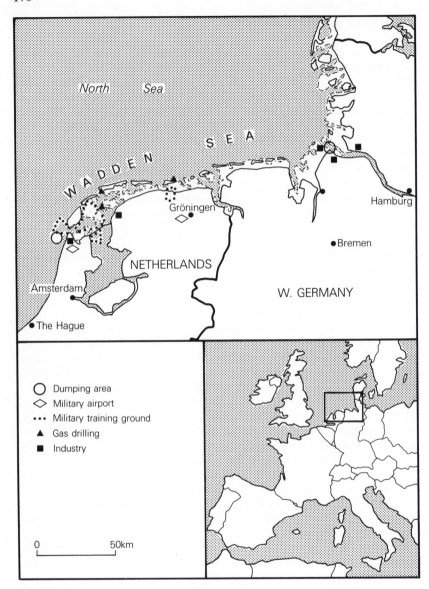

The Wadden Sea.

Carlos Quesada, head of the department of Natural Renewable Resources at CATIE (a Costa Rica-based tropical agronomy research institute), "in order to manage wetlands we need to review management of the whole watershed upon which the wetlands depend". This is true in Quesada's Central American context, where some of the most rapid deforestation in the world is likely to have as much impact on downstream and coastal wetlands as if water quality in the wetlands themselves was altered directly. But it is also true throughout the world.

The 1966 Helsinki Rules on the Uses of the Waters of International Rivers (a moral agreement between countries on the fair use of the resource) include the advice that the environmental consequences of resource development activities should be identified and considered by all the countries of the river basin sharing the resource before the final decision is taken to go ahead with development in any part of the basin. With the Mekong, though, it is assumed that development will proceed despite sometimes major wetland and environmental loss, and that the task of the Environmental Unit is to minimise or mitigate these impacts.

Despite the rhetoric, the balancing act of development benefits versus adverse effects is never given a fair hearing by the political decision-making process, because economic and natural resources are rarely measured on anything like the same terms. The productivity of natural wetland systems has a real value, which must be maintained if development is to be sustainable. For that reason alone, the potentially negative effects of development on wetlands must be considered when deciding whether a particular development project should go ahead or not, rather than simply brought in to assess how best to *minimise* the impacts.

The Wadden Sea. Europe's largest wetland, the Wadden Sea is an area of shallow water, tidal mudflats, marsh and sand, extending from the northern Netherlands along the coasts of West Germany and Denmark, separated from the North Sea by a chain of barrier islands. As with so many wetlands, its influence — especially in fisheries support — extends well beyond the immediately contiguous countries; the fishing fleets of many nations benefit from the maintenance of productivity and food chain support provided by the Wadden Sea.

The case for recognising the Wadden Sea as an international sanctuary is strong. In 1975, scientists from all three countries taking part in the Conference of Wadden Sea Experts concluded that it was only possible to "conserve the values of the Wadden Sea region by conserving the area as a whole". They pointed out the need for the three nations to develop a common policy for management; for management to be based on sound research; and for scientists, planners and politicians to cooperate in the development of sound international conventions to safeguard the wetland complex.

The Wadden Sea is the most important single wetland in western Europe. Vitally important to huge numbers of waterfowl, it also supports 80% of the North Sea's plaice, 60% of the brown shrimp, more than half the sole, and nearly all the herring. But these natural functions must compete with the exploitation of the area's large natural gas fields.

IUCN subsequently drew up a draft convention on the conservation of the Wadden Sea, which underlined the joint responsibilities of the three countries and called for closer planning cooperation. An international ad hoc working group of scientists set up in 1965 has consistently argued for coordinated management to meet the threats posed by embankments, pollution, exploitation of mineral resources, excessive recreation and tourism. Since 1963, 35,000 hectares have been reclaimed and plans for an additional 23,000 hectares are pending. This would result in the loss of saltmarshes, tidal flats and channels which are vital functional habitats.

Wadden Sea pollution comes mainly from the Scheldt, Meuse, Rhine, Ems, Weser and Elbe, and includes organic and mineral waste from the surrounding industrial regions. Chlorinated hydrocarbons, including polychlorinated biphenyls (PCBs, a class of highly toxic and long-lived industrial chemicals), are acknowledged problems; the possible effects of eutrophication are as yet poorly understood. Mineral resource exploitation includes gas and oil, sand and shell dredging. Tourism is an important source of income, but some of the most popular areas — especially sand dunes — are being disturbed and physically damaged. Management is desperately needed.

At the same time as the scientific working group was founded, the Society for Conservation of the Wadden Sea (Landelijke Vereniging tot Behoud de Waddenzee — LVBW) was set up to lobby against a local government plan to build dams from Ameland to the mainland. By increasing public awareness, lobbying politicians and exercising legal restraints, opponents stopped the plans. The society is an action group with 35,000 members and works closely with other non-governmental organisations (NGOs) in the Netherlands to discourage "invasive uses in the Wadden Sea" [229]. Since 1982, the society has been promoting international cooperation. Among the most recent concerns:

* pollution by PCBs and other chemicals from identified sources in France, West Germany, Switzerland and the Netherlands;
* proposals to build pipelines across the Wadden Sea from platforms in the North Sea to the mainland;
* plans to polder 1,000 hectares of the Noord Friesland Buitendijks (the region's most important saltmarsh area) for agriculture;
* plans to build a harbour close to Emden near the West German-Dutch border, destroying 10% of one of the last and largest brackish water areas in Europe.

In 1984, the Dutch designated the whole of the Dutch Wadden Sea a Ramsar wetland — ostensibly giving its protection international status. But this has done nothing to remove the pressures originating in other countries and little to alleviate them internally. However, it does help groups like the LVBW to lobby and to run public awareness programmes. Without the pressures of NGOs, agreements like Ramsar will simply become paper exercises.

National problems of wetland management

The management, maintenance and preservation of wetlands can only succeed if built on a strong scientific research base. The case for protecting rather than developing will succeed only if people can be convinced of the functional values; sentiment carries little weight on economic balance sheets. Elaborating and understanding the structure of wetlands and their links with the wider natural environment is a high priority for wetland scientists, particularly at the national level.

Yet we are still woefully ignorant of how wetlands function and interconnect with other elements of the environment. Wetland research has traditionally fallen into a 'grey area' between ecological, environmental, limnological, geographical and geomorphological-geological research, none of which have focused clearly on wetlands. The result has been a generally uncoordinated pattern of research, tackled from different viewpoints with very different objectives. And without a central focus, the study of wetlands has received little attention from funding sources.

But this is beginning to change as the real values of wetland ecosystems are becoming better known. For instance, wetland sites figure prominently in the US National Science Foundation's Long Term Ecological Research scheme (see Chapter 11); the Reagan administration, not noted for its strong support of environmental matters, is backing the sustained efforts of the Fish and Wildlife Service in wetland research and protection.

The case of Garaet El Ichkeul, Tunisia. A 90 sq km lake and 36 sq km of seasonally flooded marshes (fresh in winter but highly saline in summer) make up a wetland complex of international importance at Ichkeul in Northern Tunisia. The area became a national park in 1980 and is now listed under the Ramsar convention and the World Heritage Convention, and has been designated a biosphere reserve by UNESCO. Extensive areas of *Potamogeton pectinatus* in the lake support overwintering pochard, widgeon and coot. *Scirpus maritimus* in the marshland feeds a large proportion of the central European population of greylag geese. And fishing and grazing yield important resources to the local people.

But a national water resources plan aims by the year 2000 to dam and divert all six rivers feeding the Ichkeul wetlands. One of the dams, the Djoumine, is already finished and a second, the Rhezala, is nearing completion. The third and largest dam, the Sedjenane, is due to be completed before the end of the decade. In 1977, the Direction des Forets asked a multidisciplinary team from University College London (UCL), under the direction of hydrologist Dr G.E. Hollis to help prepare a management plan for the area.

The water scheme, deemed a national priority for improving urban and agricultural supplies, will cut the Ichkeul freshwater catchment supply by three-quarters. Initial research established that without compensatory management, the dams would turn Ichkeul into a highly saline lake surrounded by dry salty sebkha vegetation. It would become similar to many other sites in Tunisia and North Africa, lose its internationally important role as a freshwater site for wintering waterfowl [230] and lose productivity.

In 1977, it was concluded that Ichkeul could be conserved as a wintering ground for waterfowl only if a sluice was built to regulate freshwater outflows to the sea; releases would be allowed from the reservoirs only during very dry years. This idea was overruled by the Ministry of Agriculture because of the priority given to the alternative water needs. But a review of the UCL plan by SOGREAH, the consulting engineers appointed by the French Ministry of Environment to help the Tunisian Ministry of Agriculture with the conservation problems of Ichkeul, revealed the inadequacy of a sluice as the only conservation measure. So in 1981 a new large study was begun of the possible environmental impacts of the dams and other projects, and the design management measures needed to provide long-term conservation of the present ecosystem [231].

The study has involved the Ministry of Agriculture and outside experts from UCL, SOGREAH, CNRS Camargue and ORSTROM. So far, the work has revealed that the sluice would be effective only until the third dam is finished in 1989. Future options include an expensive $37.5-90 million plan of dividing the lake into fresh and saltwater parts.

The UCL team has built a computer model of the hydrological behaviour of the Ichkeul catchment. Simulation of lake levels has closely matched actual observed patterns, so the model provides an important tool for predicting hydrological changes if the proposed developments go ahead. Field and laboratory research allows the predictions to be translated to forecast future ecological and geomorphological patterns under different scenarios. Thus research can identify the questions that need to be asked to develop the management guidelines.

UCL has suggested five different options for managing Ichkeul. Some involve not building the last three dams or making other major hydrological adjustments, which conflicts with the Ministry of Agriculture's insistence that all the dams be built and that there be no reservoir releases. In the meantime the Ministry has decided that the sluice at least will be built and may even start operating by 1986/7. This will give 5-10 years of breathing space for further research and monitoring. Dr Hollis is cautiously optimisic that, with adequate government funding, the coordinating committee can come up with a comprehensive management scheme for Ichkeul.

Given the rising water demand from Tunisia's rapidly expanding northern cities, the government's concern for an assured water supply is understandable. But as in most other wetlands, the long-term costs of any potential scheme need to be fully evaluated and possible mitigating measures considered before going ahead. These measures then need to be implemented with full government support. Whether the information gathering and research effort will succeed in maintaining the wetland functions of Ichkeul remains to be seen. Clearly the potentially harmful ecological changes did not influence the Tunisian government's original decision to go ahead with the development scheme. But if mitigating measures are not implemented soon, this decision will be compromised by the loss not only of coastal fisheries but of a major wildlife and tourist resource.

Improving the information data base

Information about wetlands is improving all the time. The US Fish and Wildlife Service National Wetlands Inventory has compiled a computer data base on the attributes and functions of wetlands of value to Man. The annotated bibliography in the inventory synthesises information from widely scattered, specialised and often obscure scientific sources. The data base is regularly maintained and updated, and accessible with a user's handbook [232] from the National Oceanographic and Atmospheric Administration (NOAA) computer in Boulder, Colorado.

The need to improve information about wetlands of ecological importance has also led to the development of a series of directories of wetlands of international importance. Two have been completed so far: for the western Palearctic [233] and the Neotropics [234]. Volumes on the Afrotropical and Australasian regions are in progress.

These directories emphasise habitats important for waterfowl, reflecting the funding from the International Waterfowl Research Bureau (IWRB) and the strong overriding influence of Ramsar convention criteria for designation. In many respects the directories are a 'shadow list' of wetlands, all of which could be notified as Ramsar sites but which for various political and other reasons are not. The Neotropical directory lists 730 sites, low by comparison with the over 800 locations in the Western Palearctic. This reflects the relative paucity of information for large parts of South America. Each entry includes details of location, area, vegetation, land tenure and use, protection status, waterfowl and other fauna, threats, current research and conservation activity and the criteria for inclusion.

The initial data base provided by these directories is the essential starting point for the development of regional management and conservation strategies. Scott and Carbonell, authors of the directories, have used the information in their Neotropical directory to make some initial observations about the general distribution of wetlands, the level of protection, the threats, and priorities for future action [235]. They have identified 118 million hectares of wetland: 110 million hectares in South America, three million hectares each in Central America and Neotropical Mexico, and two million hectares in the Caribbean.

Almost 83 million hectares of the total wetland area is in 10 wetland systems, of which 70% is in three: the Amazon Basin, delta and adjacent Amapa coast; the Pantanal of Brazil, Bolivia and Paraguay; and the Llanos of Venezuela. About 30% of these sites have some form of protection but this amounts to only 13.5% of the total area. In any case, this is only 'paper protection' since they include some of the wetlands most seriously threatened by both current and potential development. Some threat was identified in 81% of wetlands where information was available. The greatest pressures are in the Caribbean, Central America and Mexico, where population density is greatest and much less wetland remains than in South America. Of the many types of wetlands in the Neotropical realm, Scott and Carbonell conclude, mangroves are undoubtedly the most widely threatened [236].

This type of information is vital in helping decide priorities for field action, which should ideally include:

* immediate action at seriously threatened sites;
* the development of detailed national surveys, not only of where wetlands are but of their value to society;
* a system of providing regularly updated information on the functions and value of wetlands and their contribution to sustainable development;
* basic ecological research in some of the virtually unknown wetland tracts, e.g. in the Amazon and parts of the Pantanal;
* promotion of training programmes to develop the management and technical skills for wetland maintenance.

One of the major goals of the World Conservation Strategy — launched in 1980 by IUCN, WWF and UNEP — is the integration of conservation and development to ensure that modifications to the environment secure the survival and well-being of people, while maintaining sufficient natural areas to ensure the survival of existing natural diversity. The goal of the conservation community is not to stop wetland development, but to ensure that — if done — it is carried out in a way which minimises the environmental costs. The record of wetland development to date is poor, and a major effort must now be made to learn from past mistakes.

IUCN had plans to establish in 1986 a Wetlands Data Base at its Conservation and Monitoring Centre in Cambridge, UK. This would store data on wetland values and threats, and provide governments and aid agencies with the hard up-to-date information needed to make planning decisions relating to wetlands. The data provided by the unit should, in a way not so far possible, enable planners to establish whether a proposed wetland development scheme will have excessive environmental costs and what mitigating measures used in other circumstances could reduce these costs and maximise benefits.

Training wetland scientists and managers

To succeed, protection and management schemes need suitably trained personnel. Wetland managers generally need greater interdisciplinary skills than managers of most other ecosystems, which partly explains why so little formal training is available in the area. The need is particularly acute in developing countries, where governments frequently stress the shortage of adequately trained staff as the reason for shortfalls in managing reserves and enforcing wildlife legislation.

As part of its wetlands conservation programme, WWF-IUCN is running training programmes and workshops in important wetlands, e.g. in North and West Africa and the Pantanal. But without continuing education and training programmes directly relevant to their particular wetlands and environmental context, developing countries will be unable to carry through conservation programmes, no matter how much enthusiasm and external support they begin with. More importantly, they will be unable to implement their own schemes of wetland management. Training institutions — such as those at Garoua in Cameroon and CATIE in Costa Rica — have a major responsibility for ensuring the continuity of training programmes.

Influencing governments and people: the role of NGOs

Direct lobbying of government departments, development banks, aid agencies and consultancy groups can help encourage more interest among decision-makers in the conservation of wetlands. NGOs have a key role to play in this regard, especially in increasing public awareness of wetlands, their values, functions and place in the sustainable development of the natural environment.

As Tom Stoel of the US Natural Resources Defense Council argues, development aid agencies are not just technical bodies, but are political entities which respond to the priorities of both donor and recipient countries. Conservationists have occasionally been able to influence the policies of aid agencies. Pressure from US NGOs was instrumental in the US Agency for International Development changing its policy on tropical moist forests; it now provides funding of more than $100 million for projects aimed at ensuring sustainable development of such forests, and is launching a new programme specifically designed to conserve biological diversity. This example could be followed for wetlands.

A key NGO programme is the WWF-IUCN Wetlands Programme, launched in 1985. Building on the existing work of national government organisations, such as the US Fish and Wildlife Service and Britain's Nature Conservancy Council, it plans to improve political and public knowledge about wetlands. World Wildlife Fund funded the appointment of an IUCN Wetlands Programme Officer based at the IUCN office in Switzerland, and initially is financing also a Wetlands Advisory Committee, a group of international wetlands experts appointed to guide the development of the programme.

The emphasis of projects under the programme is on arguing the importance of wetlands, showing how benefits accrue to people as well as wildlife, and how conservation can be achieved, especially within the increasingly pressurised development community. Pilot projects are concentrated in seven areas:

* *Brazil*, especially the Pantanal where a regional land-use plan, improved national park strategies and a programme for protection and management of caiman are planned;
* *Central America*, where the 108 sites of international importance are considered to be under the most intensive threats in the Neotropics, particularly from pollution and the cutting of mangroves for firewood;
* *The Sahel*, especially Senegal, Mauritania, Niger and Nigeria, where pressures of water use, overgrazing, overfishing and firewood removal threaten to destroy wetland functions that could be utilised to meet human and wildlife needs on a sustained basis;
* *Coastal West Africa*, where funds will be channelled specifically to maintain the coastal wetlands of the Banc d'Arguin in Mauritania;
* *Southern Africa*, where two projects are planned to show how development and wetland protection can work together in the Kafue Flats and Bangweulu Basin;
* *China*, where the continental importance of the country's wetlands (e.g. the crane habitat at Poyang Lake in the Yangtse

Valley) is only just being made apparent to the rest of the world through the work of Western scientists;

* *Indonesia*, which has some of the richest, untouched, and least explored wetlands, especially in Irian Jaya, where WWF and IUCN hope to establish protected areas.

These projects are in addition to the more local efforts of WWF national organisations. The programme will run from 1985 to 1987, a relatively short time in which to convince decision-makers. WWF-IUCN will obviously not save the world's wetlands single-handed. What will happen when the programme ends is unclear, but two things are certain.

First, while NGOs can promote the concept of wetland conservation and collect the necessary data, it is ultimately the responsibility of governments to put the theories into practice.

Second, if the effort does not continue beyond 1987, the agenda drawn up and actions implemented to that time will be of little more than academic value.

Conclusion

Wetlands have a poor public image. National inventories of valuable natural resources usually ignore them; for the purposes of most economic accounting, they are dismissed as a waste of space, of value only if drained and converted to dryland agriculture or other uses.

Yet they are among the earth's greatest natural assets, as this book has tried to show. Scientists have begun to appreciate the vital functions wetlands perform and the goods and services they provide. The case for protecting and managing wetlands is based not just on sentimentality or the preservation of rare species (though both arguments would be quite valid on sound social and scientific grounds). Rather, the case hinges on the very real ecological and economic benefits of wetlands.

We need to stop thinking of economics, engineering, ecology and environment as separate entities. Instead, we need to start seeing them as aspects of a single ecosystem which has to be properly managed to ensure long-term stability and sustained resource availability. For instance, replacing natural wetland flood controls with civil engineering structures is not only costly, but uses resources which might be better used elsewhere (or better not used at all). Other costs — such as the loss of wetland functions (e.g. support for fisheries) and direct and indirect environmental losses — also need to be considered. The protein produced by wetland-dependent fisheries may be harvested thousands of kilometres away, a feature which makes the problems of wetland management and land use very different from those of many other ecosystems. But such are the complexities of ecological relationships that none should ever be thought of in isolation.

It will always be difficult to measure ecological or environmental values in the same way as modern society measures and operates its economic systems. We can count the cost of replacing certain wetland functions by artificial systems — such as waste water treatment — and this argument might be used to convince politicians and decision-makers of the need to maintain wetlands. We can put a value on resources such as fisheries and grazing. But the cost of lost species, of culture and of landscape goes far beyond dollars. And here wetland survival depends on public support. Raising people's awareness of wetlands and convincing them of their real value — a process that often comes up against lifelong prejudices towards marshes, swamps and bogs — is not easy.

Media attention is one approach, but real success will come only when wetland values become part of the basic educational process — at school and within the home and work environment. It will come only with a change in social values. Scientists have a clear responsibility in this regard — a responsibility to show just how important are wetlands, and in ways which non-scientists can understand.

Wetland research is still at an early stage, but it is gaining momentum. At the same time, political support is growing. Inevitably, however, there will always be too few financial resources to protect wetlands through purchase or reimbursements to landowners for lost 'potential income'. And anyway this approach can only ever provide stop-gap or emergency measures. In the North, the natural landscape must come under the same planning ethos as that applied by state and community regulations to urban and industrial activities. If such controls are considered essential to maintain the quality of life in the built environment, why not similarly safeguard the life-supporting functions of ecosystems?

Tragically, it is already too late to save many — some might say most — of the developed world's wetlands. These have already been lost to intensified agriculture, urban expansion, industrial growth and pollution. Those of the developing world are disappearing quickly, often promoted and hastened by aid and technology from the North. This aid is often given with the highest motives of 'improving' agricultural productivity and relieving poverty and malnutrition. But 'improved' agriculture generally means more subsidised, energy intensive agriculture — depending on fertilisers, fossil fuels, and artificial water control, and sometimes geared to export markets and a cash economy rather than supplying directly and locally much-needed protein. There are inevitable environmental costs, not least to the natural productivity of wetlands replaced by dams, polders, barrages and other elements of 'development'. There are costs to long-term, renewable food support. And the consequences are often felt well beyond the frontiers of the decision-making nation.

Third World countries argue that some environmental damage is inevitable if the standard of living of their peoples is to be raised, and that it is hypocrisy for rich nation scientists to be critical. The criticism would be fair if there were no other options for the poorer countries. Here we have the nub of where wetland science must lead. It must develop management strategies which make maximum sustainable use of natural productivity. Conservation is an essential part of management. Wetland conservation does not mean setting wetlands aside in protected areas and not using them at all. Indeed, using wetlands can actually be a positive measure; because wetlands change, some would disappear altogether without active land use.

Successful management demands much more information about how wetlands actually work. This will need not just the support of individual specialists — valuable though this is — but of teams of scientists representing the wide range of expertise needed to understand and investigate the environmental and ecological complexity of wetlands (e.g. plant scientists, soil and peat specialists, hydrologists, biologists, and wildlife and range experts). In order to combine the scientific, financial and social priorities, economists, politicians, human geographers, sociologists and resource managers need to become part of an interdisciplinary team to develop and implement policy for the rational use of wetlands. Ideally, a number of such groups should be set up to represent the geographical and environmental variations in wetlands. Six groups might be the starting point: Europe/Eurasia, North America, South America, Africa, southeast Asia/Oceania, and Australia/Pacific Islands.

Each would support task forces capable of empirical research, advice to governments, development and environment agencies, implementation of management strategies and professional training of local managers, technicians and scientists. Independent of any single government (but supported through international subscription and research contracts) and coordinated through a non-political organisation such as IUCN, such groups may provide the mechanism through which presently uncoordinated individual and national effort could be directed more effectively to secure for future generations the assets of the globe's wetlands — mankind's waterlogged wealth.

184

References

1. Thompson, K.: "Primary productivity of African wetlands with particular reference to the Okavango delta" in A. Campbell (Ed.): *The Okavango delta and its future utilisation*, pp. 67-79. Proc. Symp. Gaborone, Botswana, Aug./Sept. 1976 Botswana Society, Gaborone, 1977.
2. Masefield, G.B., et al: *The Oxford book of food plants*. Oxford University Press, Oxford, 1969.
3. Koonlin, T.: "Logging the swamp for food" in Stanton, W.R. & M. Flach (Eds): Sago. *The equatorial swamp as a natural resource*, pp. 13-34. Martinus Nijhoff Publishers, Kuala Lumpur, Malaysia, 1980.
4. Raimbault, M.: "Bioconversion of starch into protein" in Stanton, W.R. & M. Flach, op. cit., pp. 222-229.
5. Dykyjova, D. & J. Kvet: "Primary productivity of freshwater wetlands" in M. Smart (Ed.): *Proc. International Conference on Wetlands and Wildfowl*. International Waterfowl Resource Bureau, Slimbridge, England, 1976.
6. Johnson, R.L.: "Timber harvest from wetlands" in Greeson, P.E., J.R. Clark, & J.E. Clark (Eds): *Wetland functions and values: the state of our understanding*, pp. 598-605. American Water Resources Association, Minneapolis, Minn., 1980.
7. Williston, H.L, F.W. Shropshire & W.E. Balmer: "Cypress is promising species for management in southern wetlands" in *Forest Farmer*, Sept. 1981.
8. De la Cruz, A.A.: *Wetland uses in the tropics and their implications on the world carbon cycle*. Unpub. mss., 1982.
9. Morton, J.F.: "Craft industries from coastal wetland vegetation" in Wiley, M.L. (Ed.): *Estuarine products*, Vol. 1, pp. 254-266. Academic Press, New York, 1976.
10. Schell, D.M.: "Carbon-13 and Carbon-14 abundances in Alachan aquatic organisms: delayed production from peat in Arctic food webs" in *Science*, pp. 1068-71. 1983.
11. Mizano, T. & S. Mori: "Preliminary Limnological Survey of some S.E. Asian Lakes". *Proc. Regional Meeting Inland Water Biologists in S.E. Asia*, pp. 105-7. UNESCO Field Office, Jakarta, 1970.
12. Macartney, C.: "These 'Wastelands' are vast storehouses" in World Wildlife Fund Wetlands Pack 2. WWF-IUCN, Gland, Switzerland, 1985.
13. Turner, R.E.: "Intertidal regulations and commercial yields of penacid shrimp". *Trans. Amer. Fish Soc.* No. 106, pp. 411-416, 1977.
14. MacIntosh, D.J.: "Riches lie in tropical swamps" in *Geographical Magazine*, Vol. LV, No. 4, pp. 184-188, April 1983.
15. Macartney, C., op. cit.
16. Ibid.
17. Christensen, B.: "Mangroves — What are they worth?" in *Unasylva*, Vol. 35, No. 139, pp. 2-15 (paper based on FAO study "Management and utilisation of mangroves in Asia and the Pacific"), 1983.
18. Pantulu, V.V.: *Effects of water resource development on wetlands in the Mekong basin*. Environment Unit, Mekong Secretariat, Bangkok. Mss., 1981.
19. Ibid.

185

20.   Welcomme, R.L.: *Fisheries of African floodplain rivers*. Longman, 1979.
21.   Ibid.
22.   Ibid.
23.   Ibid.
24.   Daget, J. (1952) quoted in Welcomme, R.L., op. cit.
25.   *Indonesian Weekly News Summary*, Indonesian Embassy, Bern, 1984.
26.   De la Cruz, A.A.: "Economic evaluations and ecological implications of alternative uses of mangrove swamps in S.E. Asia". *Proc. Asian Symp. on mangrove evaluation: research and management*, Kuala Lumpur, Malaysia. 25-29 Aug. 1980.
27.   Ling quoted by Christensen, B., op. cit.
28.   Karlsson, S. & L. Leonardson: "Extensive production and aquaculture in the Negril and Black River Lower Morasses, Jamaica; present conditions and suggestions for improvements — marketing and economic assessment of wetland resources". Appendix I to Bjork, S.: *Optimum utilization study of the Negril and Black River Lower Morasses*, Jamaica. PCJ, Kingston, 1984.
29.   Ibid.
30.   Turner, R.E.: "Protein yield from wetlands" in Gopal, B., R.E. Turner, R.G. Wetzel & D.F. Whigham (Eds): *Wetlands, ecology and management*. National Institute of Ecology and International Science Publishers, Lucknow, India, 1980.
31.   De la Cruz, A.A., op. cit.
32.   Ibid.
33.   Ibid.
34.   Cowardin, C.M., V. Carter, F.C. Golet & E.T. LaRoe: *Classification of wetlands and deepwater habitats of the United States*. US Fish & Wildlife Service, Washington DC, 1979.
35.   Hofstetter, R.H.: *Effects of fire in the ecosystem. An ecological study of the effects of fire on the wet prairie, sawgrass glades, and pineland communities of South Florida*. Report to National Park Service. University of Miami, Florida, May 1973.
36.   Egler, F.E.: "Southeast saline Everglades vegetation, Florida and its management" in *Vegetatio*, No. 3, pp. 213-265, 1952.
37.   Koonlin, T., op. cit.
38.   Harrison (1970) cited by Koonlin, T., op. cit., pp. 13-34.
39.   Essai cited in Stanton, W.R. & M. Flach, op. cit.
40.   Klotzli, F. & E. Maltby: "Mires on the move in Europe" in *Geographical Magazine*, Vol. LV, pp. 346, July 1983.
41.   Beadle, L.C.: *The inland waters of tropical Africa*. Longmans, 1974.
42.   MacIntosh, D.J., op. cit.
43.   Ibid.
44.   Christensen, B., op. cit.
45.   De la Cruz, A.A., op. cit., 1980.
46.   MacIntosh, D.J., op. cit.
47.   Ibid.
48.   Tydeman, C.: "General value of man-made wetlands for wildlife in Europe" in World Wildlife Fund Wetlands Pack 1. WWF-IUCN, Gland, Switzerland, 1984.
49.   Beebee, T.J.: "Habitats of the British amphibians: (2) suburban parks and gardens". *Biol. Cons.*, Vol. 15, pp. 241-57, 1979.
50.   Clymo, R.S. & R. Lewis-Smith: "An extraordinary peat-forming community" in *Nature*, Vol. 309, pp. 617, 1984.
51.   Richardson, C.J.: "Pocosins: vanishing wastelands or valuable wetlands?" in *BioScience*, Vol. 33, pp. 626-633, 1983.
52.   Ibid.
53.   Gribbin, John: *Carbon Dioxide, Climate and Man*. Earthscan, London and Washington, 1981.

54. See Winkler, M.G. & C.B. DeWitt: "Environmental impacts of peat mining: documentation for wetland conservation" in *Environmental Conservation* (in press); Bellamy D.J. & T. Pritchard, "Project 'Telma': A Scientific Framework for Conserving the World's Peatlands" in *Biol. Cons.* No. 5, pp. 33-40.; Bord na Mona: *Fuel peat in developing countries.* Study report prepared for the World Bank, Dublin, Ireland, 1984.

55. Maltby, E.: "Changes in microbial numbers resulting from alternative management strategies in wetland and related habitats in Southern Louisiana" in Gopal, B., R.E. Turner, R.G. Wetzel & D.F. Whigham: *Wetlands, ecology and management,* pp. 477-506. National Institute of Ecology and International Science Publishers, Lucknow, India, 1980; Maltby, E.: "The impact of severe fire on Calluna moorland in the North York moors" in *Bull. Ecol.* No. 11, pp. 683-708.

56. Richardson, C.J., op. cit.

56a. Mutanen, K. & Heiskanen, V.P.: Replacing fuelwood by sod peat or peat briquettes in cookstoves used in developing countries. Paper read at International Peat Society, Kingston, Jamaica, March 1985, and others.

57. Blackwood: *Alternative uses of peat.* Report from the Wetland Resources Sub-Committee of the National Peat Committee, Jamaica, 15 July 1983.

58. Welcomme, R.L., op. cit.

59. Edmunds, T. Owen: "Delta in the desert" in *Geographical Magazine*, pp. 324-329, 1985.

60. Welcomme, R.L., op. cit.

61. Ibid.

62. Tiner, R.W.: *Wetlands of the United States: Current Status and Trends.* US Fish and Wildlife Service, 1984.

63. Agarwal, A. et al: *Water, Sanitation, Health — for All?* Earthscan, London and Washington, 1981.

64. Richardson, C.J.: "Mechanisms controlling phosphorus retention capacity in freshwater wetlands" in *Science* No. 228, pp. 1424-7, 1985.

65. Fritz, W.R. & S.C. Helle: "Cypress wetlands as a natural treatment method for secondary effluents" in Drew, M.A. (Ed.): *Environmental quality through wetlands utilization.* Symp. Coord. Council Restoration Kissimmee R. Valley & Taylor Creek-Nubbin Slough Basin, Tallahassee, Florida, 1978.

66. Vietmeyer, N.: "Good news about a greedy plant" in *National Wildlife*, Jan. 1984.

67. Ghosh, Dhrubajyoti: *Sewage treatment fisheries in East Calcutta wetlands: low cost, resource-conserving option in environment repair.* Project report on utilisation of Calcutta's sewage, Government of West Bengal, Calcutta, India, 1983 reported by Furedy, C.: "Calcutta wetland for city sewage management and re-use" in *Environmental Cons.* 1983.

68. World Wildlife Fund: India Newsletter 46, 1983.

69. Motts, W.S. & R.H. Heely: "Wetlands and ground water" in Larson, J.S. (Ed.): *A guide to important characteristics and values of freshwater wetlands in the Northeast.* Water Resource Res. Centre, University of Massachusetts, Amherst, MA, pp. 5-8, 1973.

70. Goldsmith, E. & N. Hildyard: *The social and environmental effects of large dams.* Wadebridge Ecological Centre, Camelford, England, 1984.

71. Ludden, A.P., D.L. Frink & D.H. Johnson: "Water storage capacity of natural wetland depressions in the Devils Lake Basin of North Dakota" in *Journal of Soil and Water Conservation*, Vol. 38, No. 1, pp. 45-48, 1983.

72. US Corps of Engineers (1972) cited by Sather, J.M. & R.D. Smith in *An Overview of Major Wetland Functions and Values.* Report for US Fish and Wildlife Service, FWS/OBS-84/18, Sept. 1984.

73. Quoted in Horwitz, E.L.: *Our Nation's Wetlands.* Council on Environmental Quality, US Government Printing Office, Washington, 1978.

74. Wijkman, A. & Timberlake, L.: *Natural disasters — acts of God or acts of Man?* Earthscan, London and Washington, 1984.
75. Saenger, P., E.J. Hegerl & J.D.S. Davie: *Global status of mangrove ecosystems.* IUCN-WWF, Gland, Switzerland, 1983.
76. Keble Martin, W.: *The New Concise British Flora.* Ebury Press and Michael Joseph, London, 1982.
77. Seidensticker, J. & Md. Abdul Hai: *The Sundarbans wildlife management plan: conservation in the Bangladesh coastal zone.* IUCN, Gland, Switzerland, 1983.
78. Christensen, B., op. cit.
79. MacIntosh, D.J., op. cit.
80. Williams, J.D. & C.K. Dodd, Jr.: "Importance of wetlands to endangered and threatened species" in Greeson, P.E. et al, op. cit., pp. 565-575.
81. *Cropland or wasteland — the problems and promises of irrigation.* Earthscan Press Briefing Document 38, London and Washington, 1984.
82. World Wildlife Fund Wetlands Pack 2, op. cit.
83. Aronson, J.A.: "Economic Halophytes. A Global Review" in *Economic plants for arid lands.* Conf. Royal Botanical Gardens. Kew, 23-27 July, 1984. George Allen & Unwin, 1984.
84. Moore, N.W.: *Ramsar Conf.*, Groningen, 1984.
85. Moore, N.W.: Rep. Odon. Specialist Group IUCN 3, 1982.
86. Nurse, E.A.: "Maintaining freshwater and marine biological diversity in LDCs". Unpub. mss., 1984., reported in Wetlands Cons. Prog., WWF-IUCN, Gland, Switzerland, May 1985.
87. Welcomme, R.L., op. cit.
88. Howard, E.W. & R.C.V. Jeffery: *Kafue lechwe population status 1981-1983.* A report to the Director, National Parks and Wildlife Service, 1983.
89. Seidensticker, J. & Md. Abdul Hai, op. cit.
90. Macartney, C.: *Environmental Awareness* No. 6, 1983.
91. Skinner, J. & M. Smart: "The El Kala wetlands of Algeria and their use by waterfowl" in *Wildlife*, No. 35, pp. 106-118, 1984.
92. Carp, E.: *A Directory of Western Palaearctic Wetlands.* IUCN-UNEP Gland, Switzerland, 1980.
93. Braakhekke, W.G. & C.A. Drijver: *Wetlands: importance, threats and protection.* Dutch Society for the Protection of Birds, Zeist, Netherlands, 1984.
94. Fetherstone, R.: "Texel's devotion to nature" in *Geographical Magazine*, June 1982.
95. *The Guardian*, 6 Aug. 1985.
96. Tiner, R.W., op. cit.
97. US Dept of the Interior and Dept of Commerce, 1982.
97a. Johnson, R.L., op. cit.
98. Maltby, E.: "When the earth burns" in *Geographical Magazine*, 1984.
99. Weller, 1981; Harman, 1981, cited by Winkler, M.G. & C.B. DeWitt, op. cit.
100. Tiner, R.W., op. cit.
101. Ibid.
102. Maltby, E.: "Wetlands for the future" in *Geographical Magazine*, Vol. LV, No. 12, pp. 626-627, Dec. 1983.
103. NCC Press Notice, July 1985.
104. *IUCN Bulletin*, December, 1985.
105. Baldock, D.: *Wetland drainage in Europe.* IIED/IEEP, London, 1984.
106. Kempen, H. & J. Jansen (1982): *Drainage in the Netherlands.* Unpub. mss., quoted by David Baldock, op. cit., 1984.
107. Baldock D., op. cit., 1983.
108. Turner, R.E. & E. Maltby: "Louisiana is the Wetland State" in *Geographical Magazine*, Vol. LV, pp. 92-97, 1983.

188

109. Tiner, R.W., op. cit.
110. Morehead, J.M.: *Attempts to modify significant deterioration of a park's Natural Resource: A Case Study of Everglades National Park*, Paper to Third World National Park Congress, Bali, Indonesia, 1982.
111. Tiner, R.W., op. cit.
112. Maltby, E.: "Effects of Nutrient Loadings on Decomposition Profiles in the Water Column and submerged Peat in the Everglades". In *Proc. Int. Peat Society*, Jamaica, 1984.
113. Submission by the Aquatic Resources Division of the Natural Resources Conservation Department of Jamaica. In: Scott, D.A. & M. Carbonell: *A Directory of Neotropical Wetlands*, IUCN, Gland, Switzerland, 1985.
113a. Wade, B.: "The Black River : Waterway, Wetlands and a Way of Life" in *Jamaica Journal*, Vol. 17 pp. 10-23, Nov. 1984-Jan. 1985.
114. Nortes, M. in Scott, D.A. & M. Carbonnell, op. cit.
115. Welcomme, R.L., op. cit.
116. Bord na Mona, op. cit., 1984.
117. Armentano, T.V.: "Drainage of organic soils as a factor in the world carbon cycle" in *BioScience*, Vol. 30, pp. 825-30, 1980.
118. Scott, D.A. & M. Carbonell, op. cit.
119. Interim Committee for Coordination of Investigations of the Lower Mekong Basin. *Environmental Investigation of the Development of Water and Land Resources in the Mekong Delta, Vietnam.* Background Document MKG/R.521, June 1985.
120. Pannier, F.: "Mangroves impacted by human-induced disturbances: A case study of the Orinoco delta mangrove ecosystem" in *Environmental Management*, Vol. 3, No. 3, pp. 205-216, 1979 and F. Pannier, pers. comm., 1985.
121. Barnes, J.S.: Agricultural adaptability of wet soils of the North Carolina coastal plain, pp. 225-237, in Richardson, C.J.: "Pocosins: ecosystem processes and the influence of man on system response" in C.J. Richardson (Ed.): *Pocosin wetlands: An integrated analysis of coastal plain freshwater bogs in North Carolina*, pp. 135-151. Hutchinson Ross, Inc., Stroudsburg, PA, 1981.
122. Barber, R.T., W.W. Kirby-Smith & P.E.Parsley (1979): "Wetland alterations for agriculture", pp. 642-651 in P.E. Greeson et al, op. cit.
123. Ibid.
124. Richardson, C.J., op. cit.
125. Blake, N.M.: *Land into water — water into land.* Univ. Press of Florida, Tallahassee, 1980.
126. Conner, W.H. & J.W. Day Jr: "Productivity and Composition of a Bald Cypress — Water Tupelo Site and a Bottomland Hardwood Site in a Louisiana Swamp" in *American Journal of Botany*, Vol. 63, pp. 1354-64, 1976.
127. Richardson C.J., op. cit., 1983.
128. Lindenmuth W.D. & J.M. Vaslevich: "An Economic Analysis of Intensive Timber Management of Pocosins", pp. 270-282 in C.J. Richardson (Ed.), op. cit., 1981.
129. Hyman, R.: "Brazil wages war on Poachers" in *International Wildlife*, pp. 4-11, Jan./Feb., 1985.
130. Ibid.
131. Becker, M. & C. Yamashita in Scott, D.A. & M. Carbonell, op. cit.
132. Darby, H.C.: *The changing fenland.* Cambridge University Press, 1983.
133. Cited in Horwitz, E.L., op. cit.
134. Thompson, K.: "The ecology of peatlands in East and Central Africa and their classification for agriculture" in R.A. Robertson (Ed.): *Classification of peat and peatlands.* Proc. Symp. Comm. 1 of International Peat Society, Glasgow, September 1973. International Peat Society, Helsinki paper No. 8, pp. 60-73, 1973.
135. Berg (1950) cited by Thompson, K., op. cit., 1973.
136. Simola, H. & M. Lodenius: "Recent increase in mercury sedimentation in a forest

189

lake attributable to peatland drainage" in *Bulletin of environmental contamination and toxicology*, No. 29, pp. 298-305, 1982.; Renberg, I. & V. Segerstrom: "Application of varved lake sediments in paleoenvironmental studies" in *Wahlenbergia*, No. 7, pp. 125-133, 1981.

137. Skaggs, R.W., J.W. Gilliam & T.J. Sheets: *Effects of agricultural land development on drainage waters in North Carolina tidewater region.* Water Resource Research Institute, University of North Carolina, Raleigh, 1980.
138. Richardson, C.J., op. cit., 1983.
139. Biswas, A.K. et al (Eds): *Long Distance Water Transfers: A Chinese Case Study and International Experiences*, pp. xii. Tycooly International, Dublin, 1983.
140. Mermel, T.W.: "Major Dams of the World" in *Water, Power and Dam Construction*, No. 5, 1982.
141. Welcomme, R.L., op. cit.
141a. Bernacsek, G., pers. comm.
142. Ibid.
143. Ibid.
144. Trefethen: "Man's impact on the Columbia River" in Oglesby, R.T., C.A. Carlson & J.A. McCann: *River Ecology and Man*, pp. 77-98. New York Academic Press, New York, 1972.
145. Welcomme, R.L., op. cit.
146. Balon, E.K.: "Kariba: The Dubious Benefits of Large Dams" in *Ambio*, Vol. 1, pp. 40-48, 1978.
147. SCET-AGRI-SOGREAH-SCET-CAMEROON, Plan Directeur de l'Am énagement de la vall ée Superieure de la Benou é. Rapport de Phase 1, MEAVSB, Garoua, 1984.
148. Welcomme, R.L., op. cit.
149. Howard, E.W. & R.C.V. Jeffrey, op. cit.
150. Davies W.D.: *Louisiana Canals and their Influence on Wetland Development.* Ph. D. Louisiana State University, Baton Rouge, 1973.
151. Craig, N.J., R.E. Turner & J.W. Day, Jr: "Land Loss in Coastal Louisiana (USA)" in *Environmental Management*, No. 3, pp. 133-144.
152. Ibid.
153. Ibid.
154. Turner, R.E.: *Wetland Losses and Coastal Fisheries: An Enigmatic and Economically Significant Dependency.* Unpub. mss., Center for Wetland Resources, LSU, Baton Rouge.
155. Charnock, Anne: "A new course for the Nile" in *New Scientist*, pp. 285-288, 27 Oct. 1983.
156. Ibid.
157. Cobb, S.: "Jonglei's Fragile Ecosystem Under Threat" in *New Scientist*, pp. 287, 27 Oct. 1983.
158. Moghraby, A.L. El, & M.O. El Sammani: "On the Environmental and Socio-economic Impact of the Jonglei Canal Project, Southern Sudan" in *Environmental Conservation*, Vol. 12, pp. 41-48, 1985.
159. Ibid.
160. Angier, N.: "Now you see it, now you don't" in *Time*, 6 Aug. 1984.
161. Horwitz, E.L., op. cit.
162. Angier, N., op. cit.
163. Goldsmith, E. & N. Hildyard, op. cit.
164. Hunter, J.M., L. Rey & D. Scott: "Man-made Lakes: Man-made Diseases" in *Social Science and Medicine*, pp. 1134, No. 16, 1982.
165. Antas, P. de T.Z., F. Silva, M.A. dos S. Alves & S. de M. Lara-Resende in Scott. D.A. & M. Carbonell, op. cit.
166. Goldsmith, E. & N. Hildyard, op. cit.

167. Kalmari, A. (1982): *Energy use of peat in the world and possibilities in developing countries.* Seminar on Peat for Energy Use, 29-30 June 1982, Bandung, Indonesia, cited by Bord na Mona, op. cit., 1984.
168. Bord na Mona, op. cit., 1984.
169. Ibid.
170. Ibid.
171. Bord na Mona: *Developing Ireland's peat resources*, undated.
172. Herbst publicity material. Herbst Group, Kilpoole Hill, Wicklow, Ireland.
173. Farnham in Greeson, P.E., et al, op. cit.
174. Richardson, C.J., pers. comm., 1985.
174a. Winkler, M.G. & C.B. DeWitt, op. cit., 1985.
175. Eckholm, E., G. Foley, G. Barnard & L. Timberlake: *Fuelwood: the energy crisis that won't go away.* Earthscan, London & Washington, 1984.
176. Bord na Mona, op. cit., 1984.
177. IUCN Bulletin, No. 9, pp. 6-7.
178. Richardson, C.J., op. cit., 1983.
179. Bjork, S.: *Environmental Feasibility Study of Peat Mining in Jamaica.* University of Lund-Petroleum Corp. Jamaica, Kingston, Jamaica, 1983.
180. Bjork, S.: *Optimum Utilisation Study of the Negril and Black River Lower Morasses, Jamaica.* University of Lund-Petroleum Corp. Jamaica, Kingston, Jamaica, 1984.
181. *The Sunday Gleaner*, 1 July 1984.
182. Hon. Hugh Hart, pers. comm., 1985.
183. Miller, B.A.: *A Strategy for Coastal Wetland Development in Jamaica (A multi-use Scenario).* International Peat Symposium, Kingston, February 1985.
184. Maltby, E.: *Peat mining in Jamaica.* SIEP 2, IUCN, Gland, 1985.
185. Brouers, F.: Correspondence to the *Sunday Gleaner*, 4 Feb. 1985.
186. Grizzle, S., pers. comm., 1985.
187. Petroleum Corp. Jamaica report by Anderson, R.: *The benthic habitats offshore South West Point; in Relation to the Alignment of Colling System Pipelines from a Proposed Peat-fired Power Plant.* PCJ, Kingston, Jamaica, 1984.
188. Larson, J.S.: *Wetland value assessment: A review.* Paper read at SCOPE-UNEP workshop on "Ecosystems Dynamics in Wetlands and Shallow Water Bodies", Tallin, Estonian SSR, 3-13 August 1983.
189. McCormick, J.: *Acid Earth — the global threat of acid pollution.* Earthscan, London and Washington, DC, 1985.
190. *Wetlands: Their Use and Regulation.* US Congress, Office of Technology Assessment, Washington DC, OTA-0-206, March 1984.
191. Baldock, D., op. cit., 1984.
192. Mermet, L. cited by Baldock, D., op. cit., 1984.
193. In Baldock, D., op. cit., 1984.
194. Lesaffre (1982) cited in D. Baldock, op. cit., 1984.
195. Mermet, L.: pers. comm., 1985.
196. Baldock, D., op. cit., 1984.
197. Ibid.
198. Ibid.
199. Green, F.H.W.: "Field Under-drainage Before and After 1940" in *The Agricultural History Review*, 28 pp. 120-123, 1980.
200. Palmer, M.: *Biological Effects of Management Practices on Grazing Marshes in Britain.* Paper read at Joint meeting British Hydrological Soc., Welsh Hydrological Soc., and Inst. Biology on Management of Wetlands at The Wildfowl Trust, Slimbridge, England, 8 May 1985.
201. Williams, G, A. Henderson, L. Goldsmith, & A. Spreadborough: "Effects on birds of land drainage improvements in the North Kent Marshes" in *Wildfowl*, No. 34,

pp. 33-47, 1983.
202. Cited by Baldock, D., op. cit., 1984.
203. Darby, H.C., op. cit.
204. Ibid.
205. Ibid.
206. Whigham, D.: "The Long Wetland" in *Geographical Magazine*, Vol. LV, pp. 240-244, 1983.
207. Carp, E., op. cit.
208. Ibid.
208a. Goldsmith, E. & N. Hildyard, op. cit.
209. Herman, S.G., R.L. Garret, & R.L. Rudd: *Pesticides and the Western Grebe*. First Rochester Conference on Toxicity, University of Rochester, 4-6 June 1968.
210. Edmunds, T. Owen., op. cit.
211. Ibid.
212. Darby, H.C., op. cit.
213. Maltby, E.: Report on visit to Fiji to British Council, 1984.
214. Interim Committee for Coordination of Investigations of the Lower Mekong Basin, Environmental Programme of the Mekong Committee, December 1984.
215. Ibid.
216. Braakhekke, W.G. & C.A. Drijver, op. cit.
217. Interim Committee for Coordination of Investigations of the Lower Mekong Basin, op. cit., 1985.
218. Goode, D.: "Conservation of wetland habitats in Britain: an assessment of priorities". Paper given at meeting of Inst. of Biology, 18 March 1983, on *Wetlands Under Threat?* Natural History Museum, London.
219. O'Riordan, T. "Managing Broadland" in *Nature World*, No. 14, pp. 11-13, 1985.
220. Maltby, E.: *Soil property responses to surface treatment and assoc. management practices at Holscombe Allotment/Humbers Ball and Old Barrow Down/Hawkridge Plain*. An outline report to Exmoor National Park, 20 May 1983. Exmoor National Park, Dulverton, Somerset, UK.
221. Darby, H.C., op. cit.
222. Braakhekke, W.G. & C.A. Drijver, op. cit.
223. Japan International Cooperation Agency, 1984.
224. Dugan, P.: Mission to Nigeria, 15-22 March 1985. IUCN, Gland, Switzerland.
225. Ibid.
226. Ibid.
227. Ibid.
228. Saenger, P., E.J. Hegerl & J.D.S. Davie: *Global status of mangrove ecosystems*. IUCN, Gland, Switzerland, 1983.
229. "A tale of two wetlands" in *IUCN Bulletin*, Vol. 15, April/June 1984.
230. Hollis, G.E.: *The modelling and management of the internationally important wetland at Gavaet el Ichkeul, Tunisia*. Mss., Ecology and Cons. Unit, UCL, London, April 1985; and Hollis, G.E., C.T. Agnew & A.C. Stevenson: "Wildfowl damned" in *Geographical Magazine*, Vol. LVll, pp. 584, Nov. 1985.
231. Hollis, G.E., op. cit.
232. US Fish and Wildlife Service: *User's Handbook for the Wetland Values Database: 1984 Update*. Department of the Interior, 1984.
233. Carp, E., op. cit.
234. Scott, D.A. & M. Carbonell, op. cit.
235. Scott, D.A. & M. Carbonell: "The IWRB/ICBP Neotropical Wetland Project" in *Report of the XXXI Annual Meeting IWRB*, Caracus, Peru, 10-16 February 1985.
236. Ibid.

Further reading

ADAMUS, P.R. & L.T. Stockwell: *A Method for Wetland Functional Assessment*. Report No. FHWA-IP-82-23. US Dept Transportation Federal Highway Administration, Washington DC, 1983.

BLAKE, N.M.: *Land into water — water into land*. Florida State University, Tallahassee, US, 1980.

CHAPMAN, V.J.: *Wet Coastal Ecosystems*. Elsevier, Amsterdam, 1977.

COMMITTEE FOR COORDINATION OF INVESTIGATIONS OF THE LOWER MEKONG BASIN. *Annual Report*, 1984.

DRIJVER, C.A & M. Marchand.: *Taming the floods. Environmental aspects of floodplain development in Africa*. Centre for Environmental Studies. State University of Leiden, 1985.

ETHERINGTON, J.R.: *Wetland Ecology*. Edward Arnold, London, 1983.

FRITZ, W.R. & S.C. Helle: "Cypress wetlands as a natural treatment method for secondary effluents" in M.A. Drew (Ed.): *Environmental quality through wetlands utilisation*. Coordinating Council on the Restoration of the Kissimmee River Valley and Taylor Creek — Nubbin Slough Basin. Tallahassee, Florida, 1978.

GODWIN, H.: *The Archives of the Peat Bogs*. Cambridge University Press, Cambridge, 1981.

GOOD, R.E., D.F. Whigham & R.C. Simpson: *Freshwater Wetlands*. Academic Press, New York, 1978.

GORE, A.J.P. (Ed.): *Ecosystems of the World. Mires: swamp, bog, fen and moor*. Elsevier, Amsterdam, 1983.

GOSSELINK, J.G. & R.H. Baumann: *Wetlands Inventories: wetland loss along the United States coast*. Z. Geomorph. N.F. Suppl. Bd. 34, pp. 173-187, 1980.

GOSSELINK, J.G. & R.E. Turner: "The role of hydrology in freshwater wetland ecosystem", pp. 63-78 in R.E. Good et al (Eds): *Freshwater wetlands: Ecological Processes and Management Potential*. Academic Press, New York, 1978.

HAMILTON, L.S. & S.C. Snedaker (Eds): *Handbook for Mangrove Area Management*. UNEP-East-West Centre-IUCN, 1984.

HASLER, A.D.: *Coupling of land and water systems*. Springer, Berlin, 1975.

IUCN-UNEP-WWF: *World Conservation Strategy*. IUCN, Gland, Switzerland, 1980.

KIENITZ, G.: *Hydrological Regime as Influenced by Drainage of Wetlands*. UNESCO, Paris, 1979.

KUSLER, J.A.: *Strengthening State Wetland Regulations*. US Fish & Wildlife Service, FW 5/OB5-78/98, Washington DC, 1978.

KUSLER, J.A.: *Our National Wetland Heritage. A Protection Guidebook*. Environmental Law Institute, Washington DC, 1983.

LINDALL, W.N. & C.H. Saloman: "Alteration and Destruction of Estuaries Affecting Fishery Resources of the Gulf of Mexico" in *Marine Fisheries Review Paper* 1262, Vol. 39, No. 9, Sept. 1977.

LOWE-McCONNELL, R.H.: *Fish Communities in Tropical Freshwater*. Longman, London, 1975.

LUGO, A.E. & S.C. Snedaker: "The Ecology of Mangroves" in *A. Rev. Ecol. Syst.* 5, pp. 39-64, 1974.

MITCH, W.J. & J.G. Gosselink: *Wetlands*. Van Rostrand Reinhold Co., New York, 1986.

MOSS, B.: *Ecology of Freshwaters*. Blackwell, Oxford, 1980.

NATURE CONSERVANCY COUNCIL: *The future of Broadland*. Nature Conservancy Council, Norwich, UK, June 1977.

NEWTON, R.B.: *New England Wetlands: A Primer*. University of Massachusetts, Amherst, MS Thesis, 1981.

PANTULU, V.R.: *Fishery Problems and Opportunities in the Mekong*. Geophysical Monograph Series 17, pp. 672-682, 1973.

RANWELL, D.S.: "World Resources of *Spartina townsendii* (s. lat) and economic use of *Spartina* marshland" in *J. App. Ecol.* 4, pp. 239-56.

SATHER, J.H. & R.D. Smith: *An overview of major wetland functions*. US Fish & Wildlife Service, FWS/OBS-84/18. US Dept Interior, Washington DC, 1984.

SCUDDER, T. & T. Conelly: "Management systems for riverine fisheries" in *FAO Fish. Tech. Pap.* (263), 1985.

SIMPSON, R.L., R.E. Good, M.A. Leck & D.F. Whigham: "The ecology of freshwater tidal wetlands" in *BioScience* Vol. 33, pp. 255-259.

SLACK, A.: Carnivorous Plants. Ebury Press, London, 1979.

SMALL, M: *Meadow/Marsh Systems as Sewage Treatment Plants*. Brookhaven National Laboratory, Upton, New York, 1972.

STANLEY, H.F. & M.P. Alpers: *Man-made lakes and human health*. Academic Press, London, 1975.

THOMPSON, K. & A.C. Hamilton: "Peatlands and Swamps of the African Continent" in A.J.P. Gore (Ed.), op. cit., 1983.

TURNER, R.E. & N.J. Craig: "Recent areal changes in Louisiana's forested wetland habitat" in *Proc. of the Louisiana Acad. Sci.*, Vol. XL, pp 61-68, 1980.

US ENVIRONMENTAL PROTECTION AGENCY: *Freshwater wetlands for wastewater management*. Report No. EPA 094/9-83-107, Atlanta, GA, 1983.

US OFFICE OF TECHNOLOGY ASSESSMENT: *Wetlands: their use and regulation*. US Congress, Office of Technology Assessment, OTA-0-206, March 1984.

WILEY, M.: *Estuarine Processes*, Vol. 1. Academic Press, New York, 1976.

WOLVERTON, B.C. & R.C. McDonald: *Water Hyacinths for Upgrading Sewage Lagoons to Meet Advanced Wastewater Treatment Standards*. NASA Technical Memorandum, St Louis, Miss. US, 1978.

WWF-IUCN: *Wetlands Conservation Programme 1985-87. Life at the Water's Edge*. WWF-IUCN, Gland, Switzerland, 1985.

ZINN J.A. & C. Copeland: *Wetland management*. Congressional Research Service Report. Ser. No. 97-11, US Library of Congress, Washington DC, 1982.

194

Index

EARTHSCAN PAPERBACKS

A Village in a Million by Sumi Krishna Chauhan   1979
£2.00/$5.00

Mud, mud — The potential of earth-based materials for Third World housing by Anil Agarwal   1981   £2.50/$5.50   Also in French & Spanish

Water, Sanitation, Health — for All? Prospects for the International Drinking Water Supply and Sanitation Decade, 1981-90 by Anil Agarwal, James Kimondo, Gloria Moreno and Jon Tinker   1981
£3.00/$5.50

Fuel Alcohol: Energy and Environment in a Hungry World by Bill Kovarik   1982   £3.00/$5.50

Stockholm Plus Ten: Promises, Promises? The decade since the 1972 UN Environment Conference by Robin Clarke and Lloyd Timberlake   1982   £3.00/$5.50

Tropical Moist Forests: The Resource, The People, The Threat by Catherine Caufield   1982   £3.00/$5.50   Also in French & Spanish

What's wildlife worth? by Robert and Christine Prescott-Allen   1982   £3.00/$5.50   Also in Spanish

Desertification — how people make deserts, how people can stop and why they don't by Alan Grainger   1982   £3.00/$5.50   Also in French

Gasifiers: fuel for siege economies by Gerald Foley, Geoffrey Barnard and Lloyd Timberlake   1983   £3.00/$5.50

Genes from the wild — using wild genetic resources for food and raw materials by Robert and Christine Prescott-Allen   1983
£3.00/$5.50

A million villages, a million Decades? The World Water and Sanitation Decade from two South Indian villages —

Guruvarajapalayam and Vellakal by Sumi Krishna Chauhan and K. Gopalakrishnan   1983   £3.00/$5.50

Who puts the water in the taps? Community participation in Third World drinking water, sanitation and health by Sumi Krishna Chauhan with Zhang Bihua, K. Gopalakrishnan, Lala Rukh Hussain, Ajoa Yeboah-Afari and Francisco Leal   1984   £3.00/$5.50

Stoves and trees by Gerald Foley, Patricia Moss and Lloyd Timberlake   1984   £3.50/$5.50

Fuelwood: the energy crisis that won't go away by Erik Eckholm, Gerald Foley, Geoffrey Barnard and Lloyd Timberlake   1984   £3.50/$5.50

Natural disasters: Acts of God or acts of Man? Anders Wijkman and Lloyd Timberlake   1984   £3.50/$5.50   Also in Spanish

Urban land and shelter for the poor by Patrick McAuslan   1985   £3.50/$5.50   Also in Spanish

Africa in crisis — the causes, the cures of environmental bankruptcy by Lloyd Timberlake   1985   £3.95/$6.25, Hardback £9.95/$16.00

Acid earth — the global threat of acid pollution by John McCormick   1985   £3.95/$6.25

All Earthscan publications are available from:

Earthscan   Earthscan Washington
3 Endsleigh Street   1717 Massachusetts Avenue NW
London WC1H ODD, UK   Washington DC 20036, USA